T0361290

Cambridge Elements ☰

Elements in Corpus Linguistics
edited by
Susan Hunston
University of Birmingham

SHAPING WRITING GRADES

Collocation and Writing Context Effects

Lee McCallum
Coventry University

Philip Durrant
University of Exeter

CAMBRIDGE
UNIVERSITY PRESS

University Printing House, Cambridge CB2 8BS, United Kingdom

One Liberty Plaza, 20th Floor, New York, NY 10006, USA

477 Williamstown Road, Port Melbourne, VIC 3207, Australia

314–321, 3rd Floor, Plot 3, Splendor Forum, Jasola District Centre,
New Delhi – 110025, India

103 Penang Road, #05–06/07, Visioncrest Commercial, Singapore 238467

Cambridge University Press is part of the University of Cambridge.

It furthers the University's mission by disseminating knowledge in the pursuit of
education, learning, and research at the highest international levels of excellence.

www.cambridge.org
Information on this title: www.cambridge.org/9781009074445
DOI: 10.1017/9781009070461

© Lee McCallum and Philip Durrant 2022

First published 2022

A catalogue record for this publication is available from the British Library.

ISBN 978-1-009-07444-5 Paperback
ISSN 2632-8097 (online)
ISSN 2632-8089 (print)

Shaping Writing Grades

Collocation and Writing Context Effects

Elements in Corpus Linguistics

DOI: 10.1017/9781009070461
First published online: July 2022

Lee McCallum
Coventry University

Philip Durrant
University of Exeter

Author for correspondence: Lee McCallum, lee.mccallum@coventry.ac.uk

Abstract: This Element explores relationships between collocations, writing quality, and learner and contextual variables in a first-year composition (FYC) programme. Comprising three studies, this Element is anchored in understanding phraseological complexity and its sub-constructs of sophistication and diversity. First, the authors look at sophistication through association measures. They tap into how these measures may tell us different types of information about collocation via a cluster analysis. Selected measures from this clustering are used in a cumulative links model to establish relationships between these measures, measures of diversity and task, the language background of the writer and individual writer variation, and writing quality scores. A third qualitative study of the statistically significant predictors helps understand how writers use collocations and why they might be favoured or downgraded by raters. This Element concludes by considering the implications of this modelling for assessment.

Keywords: collocation, phraseological complexity, writing quality, mixed models, first year-writing

ISBNs: 9781009074445 (PB), 9781009070461 (OC)
ISSNs: 2632-8097 (online), 2632-8089 (print)

Contents

1 Introduction

Holistic marking is often the norm for assessing essays in academic contexts. An on-going question is what makes a rater give higher or lower marks to different essays. This Element aims to gain an understanding of the linguistic and non-linguistic variables that may play a role in shaping the writing quality scores awarded to student essays by raters. Our work answers one central question: what linguistic and non-linguistic variables may play a role in shaping the writing quality scores awarded to student essays in a first-year composition (FYC) writing context?

The underlying premise is that collocation may play a role in understanding what shapes writing quality scores. We also assume that non-linguistic factors such as variation in individual writers, the writing task, and the language status of the writers may play a role in shaping scores.

To understand these variables, our work engages with the following methodologically driven sub-questions:

(i) How can we choose appropriate measures of collocation?
(ii) How can we measure and understand the potential role of different linguistic and non-linguistic variables involved in shaping writing quality scores in an appropriate way?

By answering these questions, we hope to illuminate the complexity of the linguistic and non-linguistic variables themselves, as well as how these variables operate with a degree of nuance in the rating process overall. We hope to illuminate, and to some extent demystify, different aspects of the rating process in a relatively underexplored FYC writing context in the United States (see Section 2 for details of the writing context).

Three empirical studies are carried out to answer these questions. The first question is answered by engaging with past literature and through the study of collocation measures in a cluster analysis. The second question is answered via the use of a cumulative-link mixed effects regression model. This model can accommodate different variable types to appreciate how they may play a role in shaping writing scores. A follow-up qualitative study provides a deeper understanding of how writers use collocations in their writing and also helps answer the second question.

The introductory section of this Element presents the rationale for the focus on these particular questions and our methods for answering them.

1.1 Understanding Writing Quality via Quantitative Linguistic Features

There has been a long-standing interest in understanding rater judgements of writing quality in first and second language research. This interest has adopted several theoretical and methodological lenses (e.g., see the overview in Durrant et al., 2021). One popular lens used to tap into these judgements and the inferences we can (and cannot) make from them has been the quantitative study of the relationship between linguistic features and writing quality grades. Under this lens, linguistic features are identified (normally by adhering to a specific theoretical framework that governs how to identify the features) and counted (manually or automatically with corpus software), and then relationships between these frequencies and writing quality grades are established numerically using statistical techniques such as correlation and regression analyses. Writing quality grades represent subjective ratings made by text evaluators who largely make their judgements from a predetermined set of criteria which to an extent presupposes what 'good' writing involves. These criteria therefore guide evaluators in their judgements (e.g., see the IELTS and TOEFL grade bandings mentioned in Durrant et al., 2021). This quantitative approach has enjoyed sustained popularity in the literature and is currently experiencing something of a 'boom', thanks to the increasing creation of corpus software tools which make the counting and analyses of such features increasingly user-friendly. This boom is well documented across overviews provided in Durrant et al. (2021) and Crossley (2020).

In their studies, researchers make two key assumptions. First, there is an assumption of, or perhaps appreciation for, the role that linguistic features themselves may play in our understandings of writing quality judgements as a measurable construct. This means there is an underlying belief that by counting linguistic features and looking at their relationships with writing quality via statistical methods, we can learn something about how these features may be being judged/perceived by raters. Second, and linking back to the first assumption, is the belief that the linguistic features chosen are (a) worth counting (because they have an established linguistic history/history in models of writing proficiency/quality), and (b) that they can indeed be reliably counted.

Findings of past feature-writing quality work have gone on to inform two often connected areas of research: the development of writing proficiency scales/ rubrics by referring to differences in linguistic feature use across bandscales (e.g., Hawkins & Filipovic, 2012), and/or the training of large-scale feedback and grading systems (e.g., Chen et al., 2017). Researchers have most persistently studied features of grammar (e.g., clauses (see Bulté & Housen, 2014)) and vocabulary (e.g., percentage of words appearing in the Academic Word List (Daller et al., 2013)), with features of cohesion occupying an inconsistent position of interest for researchers (e.g., see the review in Durrant et al. (2021)). Features of phraseology, for example lexical bundles (e.g., see Appel & Wood, 2016), occupy an increasingly prominent position, especially in second language litera- ture (e.g., see reference made to this emerging importance in Durrant et al. (2021) and Paquot (2018, 2019)).

It is this latter linguistic area that this Element focusses on. The following sub-sections make an explicit case for the study of one specific area of phrase- ology: that of collocation. The sub-sections present the rationale for such a focus and explain how this Element contributes to understanding the role collocation may play alongside several non-linguistic writing assessment vari- ables in shaping writing quality judgements.

1.2 The Rationale for Studying Collocations and Writing Quality

The use of appropriate language is viewed as a key component of success for meeting programme outcomes in the FYC programme our Element focusses on (CWPA, 2014; CWPA et al., 2011). In this sense, using appropriate academic language is therefore a requirement of fitting into students' respective academic disciplines/communities. Wray (2006, p. 593) notes on this matter that 'when we speak, we select particular turns of phrase that we perceive to be associated with certain values, styles and groups', with the learning of these phrases or word combinations acting as a badge of identity and this badge is linked to particular academic communities.

Later, Wray (2019, p. 267) emphasises that the status of a word combination as a formula lies in the decision-making or perceptions of the agent. She states that a formulaic sequence is 'any multiword string that is perceived by the agent (i.e., learner, researcher, etc.) to have an identity or usefulness as a single lexical unit'. Siyanova-Chanturia and Pellicer-Sánchez (2019, p. 6) highlight that there are several frameworks or reasons that guide the perceiver's decision-making. It may entail high frequency of occurrence (since frequently produced strings, other than being useful by virtue of being frequent in language, may also benefit from being treated as a single unit), a teacher's perceived value of a string (no matter how frequent), some sort of basic holistic storage and processing, a specific pragmatic function, or, indeed, something altogether different.

Although these definitions allow researchers flexibility in their theoretical and methodological approaches to capturing formulas, two particular approaches have dominated the literature: phraseological and frequency-based approaches (see Nesselhauf (2005) for an in-depth overview of the differences between these lenses). This Element grounds its theoretical and methodological conceptualisation of collocation in the frequency-based lens. Under a frequency-based lens, the tenets of collocation rest on understandings from Firth (1968, p. 181), who believed that part of a word's meaning is the 'habitual collocations' in which it appears. Meaning here is said to include both the concept with which the word is associated and the ways in which it is used. Firth (1968) gives the example of '*dark night*', resting his understanding on the belief that collocating words are part of each other's meaning. Thus, because *dark* appears frequently alongside *night*, collocability with *night* is one of the meanings of *dark* (Firth, 1957, p. 196). Later, Firth (1968) articulates these thoughts further to indicate that collocation is a type of mutual expectancy between words. Collocating words are said to predict each other, in the sense that the presence of one word makes the presence of the other more likely.

Corpus linguists have unpacked this mutual expectancy further by stating that collocation is 'the relationship a lexical item has with items that appear with greater than random probability in its (textual) context' (Hoey, 1991, p. 7), with Jones and Sinclair (1974) simply stating that words are collocates if they appear together more frequently than their individual word frequencies would predict. Under these views, there is also a psycholinguistic nature to collocation to consider, with Sinclair's (1987, p. 391) idiom principle setting out this mental association where 'a language user has available to him or her a large number of semi-preconstructed phrases that constitute single choices, even though they might appear to be analysable into segments'. Further still, Hoey's (2005, pp. 3–5) theory of lexical priming also draws attention to the psycholinguistic nature of collocation in that it is seen as the 'psychological association between words … evidenced by their occurrence together in corpora more often than is explicable in terms of random distribution'. Under these guiding thoughts then, collocation is bound up in the idea that word combinations are more frequent than their individual word frequencies would explain and that there is a degree of non-random use to these pairings.

These thoughts have led researchers to develop multiple taxonomies and dictionaries of collocations (e.g., Benson et al., 2009) with studies presenting word combinations such as (i) '*heavy rain*', (ii) '*rancid butter*', and (iii) '*apologise profusely*', as collocations (e.g., Paquot, 2018). Under the frequency-based school of thought, researchers have commonly captured collocations like these by focussing on the belief that collocations are pairs of words which regularly co-occur within a given span or window of text, for example two to four words either side of the node/search word. This approach has been criticised as capturing syntactically unrelated or uninteresting collocations (e.g., Evert, 2009). More recently a smaller group of studies have identified collocations using syntactic parsers which capture collocations according to a particular syntactic dependency relationship. Dependency pairings are decided by parsing a text using an automated parser. Dependency grammar operates on the notion that in every sentence each word is dependent on another, apart from the root of the sentence which is independent (Debusmann, 2000). A word depends on another if it is a complement or a modifier of the latter. For example, dependency pairings which might be collocations include an adjective modifying a noun.

1.2.1 The Study of Collocation in Student Writing

After using a span or syntactic approach, many researchers have focussed on studying the often-arbitrary partnering and the degree of exclusivity in combinations extracted. 'Arbitrariness' here refers to the way that collocational preferences can sometimes appear to defy logical explanation. For example, the fact that an idea can be 'utterly ridiculous' but not 'utterly sensible'. 'Exclusivity' refers to the way that some words are found almost exclusively in combination with another particular word, or group of words. For example, the fact that few things other than 'rain' can be described as 'torrential' and that few things can be 'shrugged' other than our 'shoulders'. It is these often arbitrary, complex, and exclusive relationships that researchers have attempted to study in learner writing.

Many of the foundations for studying collocation in learner writing stem from the belief that second language learner writers struggle to use collocations appropriately. This is because the combinations are assumed to be stored mentally as single units and must be used appropriately with an understanding of their arbitrary combinatory nature and intended, expected meaning. However, there is growing evidence that first language learners also struggle with collocation. They struggle to navigate the expected writing of university genres and disciplines for the first time. Both groups therefore encounter barriers in using the language expected and ultimately gaining acceptance, through that language use, into their academic communities (Durrant, 2019; Wray, 2002).

Under a frequency-based approach, scholars have used frequency information to statistically show two pieces of information about learner collocation: (i) how confident we can be that the word combination does or does not occur because of random chance and (ii) the degree of exclusivity the words in the combination have with each other; in other words – the degree to which they may in fact have other possible combinatory partners. The formulae used to capture these are known as association measures (Evert, 2004).

Evert (2004, p. 75) defines an association measure as 'a formula that computes an association score from the frequency information in a pair's contingency table'. A contingency table is a 2 × 2 table that lays out a word combination's frequency information. The table contains frequency information relating to the frequency of the combination, the frequency of word 1 and word 2 in the pair, the frequency of other possible word combinations using either word 1 or 2, and the size of the reference corpus being used. An illustration of a contingency table is provided in Brezina et al. (2015, pp. 144–5). Evert (2004) groups measures able to capture confidence as (i) significance measures, and those able to capture exclusivity as measures of (ii) association strength. These types of information have been interpreted as the higher the score, the more confident we can be that the combination is a collocation (i.e., not occurring because of random chance) in (i), and in (ii), the higher the score, the more exclusive the pairing and the less likely it is to have multiple other word partners that it pairs with naturally.

Those researching learner writing have mostly relied on two representative measures from the significance and the degree of strength groups. In the former, this has been the t-score, and in the latter, the mutual information (MI) score. The t-score, as a measure of confidence, has been found to flag up word combinations that comprise high-frequency words (e.g., 'little bit', 'other hand') (Granger & Bestgen, 2014). In contrast, the MI has been found to flag up word combinations that comprise low-frequency words (which make them more exclusive to each other). For example, 'tectonic plate' and 'juvenile delinquency' (Durrant & Schmitt, 2009; Granger & Bestgen, 2014).

Several studies have used these measures to inform understandings of second language learner writing (e.g., Bestgen, 2017; Bestgen & Granger, 2014; Chen, 2019; Durrant & Schmitt, 2009; Garner et al., 2019, 2020; Granger & Bestgen, 2014; Kim et al., 2018), with few studies of first language learner writing (e.g., Durrant & Brenchley, 2021; Kyle et al., 2018). In their English for Academic Purposes (EAP) study, Durrant and Schmitt (2009) found that second language writers used more high-scoring t-score combinations, while first language writers used more high-scoring MI combinations (more exclusive pairings found in discipline- and genre-specific writing). To some extent, this finding has been corroborated in other second language contexts (e.g., Bestgen, 2017; Bestgen & Granger, 2014; Garner et al., 2019, 2020; Granger & Bestgen, 2014); however, across these individual contexts, increases in MI combination use have not always been linear across year groups of learners or proficiency levels (e.g., Durrant & Brenchley, 2021; Paquot, 2018, 2019).

1.3 Emerging Questions from Current Studies

1.3.1 How Can We Choose Appropriate Measures of Collocation?

The first question that this Element engages with is 'How can we choose appropriate measures of collocation'? Engaging with this important question is warranted because, as previous sections of the Element have noted, past studies have raised several issues relating to the use of association measures. Scholars have relied on a narrow set of measures that have been restricted to association measures used in the language learning/assessment literature with the t-score and MI featuring prominently. There has been sparse mention of alternatives or an awareness of how the hundreds of other association measures touted in the literature align with the MI or t-score or may be able to illuminate different collocation properties to those highlighted by the MI and t-score (e.g., see criticisms in Öksuz et al. (2021) and acknowledgement of the hundreds of measures in Pecina (2005, 2010), Wiechmann (2008), Gries and Ellis (2015), and more recently Kyle et al. (2018) and Kyle and Eguchi (2021)). This Element's starting position is that the use of these measures needs to be understood against the wider bank of association measures that researchers have access to. The measures need to be understood in terms of their ability to illuminate different types of collocation properties. There is also a need to bring together the fragmented association measure literature. This fragmented picture means measurement choice is often underexplored and/or undertheorised because measures are spread out across different disciplines and scholars (Öksuz et al., 2021).

1.3.2 How Can We Measure and Understand the Potential Role of Different Linguistic and Non-linguistic Variables Involved in Shaping Writing Quality Scores in an Appropriate Way?

The second question that this Element engages with is 'How can we measure and understand the potential role of different linguistic and non-linguistic variables involved in shaping writing quality scores in an appropriate way'? Studies in this research area have started to use a wider range of statistical methods, such as recently mixed/multi-effects models (e.g., Garner et al., 2019, 2020; Paquot, 2018, 2019), to measure relationships between collocations and writing quality. Thus, a key goal of the Element is to explore how these types of models offer an appropriate method of studying writing quality scoring.

1.4 The Organisation of the Element

This Element proceeds by providing an overview of the FYC context in Section 2. Section 3 then guides readers through the current collocation-grade landscape and emphasises how the empirical work in the Element adds to this landscape. Section 4 sets out the methodological steps taken in the three individual studies. Then, Section 5 describes the results of the cluster analysis carried out to answer the first question, while Section 6 describes the results of the mixed effects modelling, carried out to partially answer the second question. Section 7 also helps answer the second question by qualitatively unpacking the possible reasons for the statistical relationships between the measures of collocation and writing quality by looking at text samples from the FYC corpus itself. Section 8 concludes the Element by summing up the key findings and limitations, and importantly how we reflect on our methodological approach and its promise in future work.

2 FYC Programmes and the Writing Context

2.1 Overview of the Section

This section will explain the rationale for focussing on a FYC programme in the United States. The section will explain how these programmes may benefit from closer engagement with language instruction. We chose to base our study on the programme at the University of South Florida (USF) because of its focus on different writing tasks.

2.2 The Nature of the FYC Programme at USF

The University of South Florida is a large public university with a diverse student population. Of its 50,000 students, as many as 41 per cent identify as African American, Black, Asian American, Hispanic, Native American, or multiracial (USF, 2018). The university provides degrees in business, engineering, arts and social sciences, and interdisciplinary sciences (USF, 2018).

As a state requirement, students who enter a Florida College or University State system have been required since 2015–16 to complete thirty-six hours of general education coursework from a list of courses in communication, mathematics, social sciences, humanities, and natural science, among others. This requirement means students develop the academic and numeracy skills needed for the demands of university study.

In the FYC programme, students complete writing as a 'process'. They develop strategies in pre-writing, co-authoring, revising, and editing, as well as learning to follow academic/disciplinary conventions for different genres. They must achieve a minimum C-grade to continue their studies.

The programme's learning objectives are set out across two modules: ENC (English Composition) 1101 and ENC 1102. Some of these objectives include the following:

- Learning and applying strategies to facilitate a range of skills, including critical reading, the stages of process writing, and giving peer feedback.
- Composing academic genres and adhering to academic conventions (structure, citation, and linguistic features).
- Synthesising disparate or conflicting thoughts when evaluating questions/problems to form cohesive and collaborative solutions.

2.2.1 Individual Project Information

Students complete six projects: three on each module. They produce drafts, carry out peer review activities, and develop a revision plan from this feedback. Across the two modules, students choose a controversial topic that they explore from different stakeholder perspectives. In ENC 1101, the three projects are: producing an annotated bibliography, analysing a stakeholder's platform, and synthesising multiple perspectives in the form of a literature review. In ENC 1102, the three projects are: developing a Rogerian argument on common ground between stakeholders and how they can compromise, analysing a visual rhetoric, and finally composing a multimodal argument in the final project.

Course ENC 1101 focusses on solidifying writing practices by introducing and practising paraphrasing, citing sources, drafting and editing work, peer review, and collaboration. Course ENC 1102 focusses more on developing students' argumentation and reasoning skills as well as their agency. Project 1 from ENC 1102 requires students to develop arguments that look at differences in stakeholder views for their chosen topics and explore how these stakeholders may reach a compromise. This project builds on Project 3 from ENC 1101, which sets out the key arguments for each stakeholder.

2.3 Teaching, Evaluation, and Feedback at USF

Modules are taught by permanent staff, adjunct instructors, and Graduate Teaching Assistants (GTAs). The ethos on the programme is that writing is constructed at a community level. This means peer review and teacher-led writing conferences feature heavily. Writing is commented on and evaluated using 'My Reviewers', a bespoke learning management system (LMS) which allows instructors and students to view programme material, draft and final projects, and to give peer and instructor feedback via PDF annotation tools.

Each of the six projects is worth between 20 and 30 per cent of students' overall grade. Students are awarded the remaining percentage of their grade for

Table 1 Holistic grades awarded for ENC 1101 and ENC 1102

Grade Types	Grade Breakdown for ENC 1101 and ENC 1102		
A	A+ (97–100) GPA: 4.00	A (94–96.9) GPA: 4.00	A– (90–93.9) GPA: 3.67
B	B+ (87–89.9) GPA: 3.33	B (84–86.9) GPA: 3.00	B– (80–83.9) GPA: 2.67
C	C+ (77–79.9) GPA: 2.33	C (74–76.9) GPA: 2.00	C– (70–73.9) GPA: 1.67
D	D+ (67–69.9) GPA: 1.33	D (64–66.9) GPA: 1.00	D– (60–63.9) GPA: 0.67
F	F (59.99 or below) 0.00		

homework tasks and class participation, equalling 100 per cent. Projects are evaluated using custom-made rubrics which instructors are trained to use. These rubrics evaluate projects according to analysis, use of evidence, organisation, focus, and style. An overall holistic grade out of fifteen points is awarded, expressed by the letters A–F. These bandings are shown in Table 1.

2.4 Language Instruction in FYC Programmes

2.4.1 The Focus on Language Instruction in FYC Programmes

Although the CWPA Outcomes Statement (2014) helps standardise FYC programmes across universities, Eckstein and Ferris (2018) highlight how the statement and the Conference on College Composition and Communication's fluid guidance on students' linguistic needs means there is the potential for explicit language input to be overlooked in favour of a focus on traditional composition processes. Indeed, several scholars have started to draw attention to the lack of language focus on FYC programmes (e.g., Matsuda et al., 2013). They acknowledge that this lack of language instruction is common despite many raters downgrading coursework because of language problems.

The CWPA Outcomes Statement (2014) makes most specific reference to language instruction on FYC programmes under its 'Rhetorical Knowledge' and 'Knowledge of Conventions' sections. When developing rhetorical knowledge, students are expected to develop the ability to respond to a variety of different contexts, that is, they must be able to shift tone, level of formality, medium, and/or structure. Instructors are expected to guide students towards learning about the main features of genres.

Despite these connections to language use, Aull (2015) emphasises that most FYC programmes focus on process pedagogies and neglect focussing on how language use facilitates meeting many of the FYC programme goals (e.g., genre and readership awareness).

2.4.2 The Focus on Language Instruction at USF

There is a strong ethos of focussing on the processes of writing and social text creation, but some attention is paid to language development. My Reviewers facilitates a focus on language through its multimedia library containing 'community' comments, a bank of more than 200 instructor-created comments that offer advice on grammar and mechanics, and resources that address different types of writing concerns (e.g., word choice/diction, weak argumentation, and logical organisation) (Moxley & Eubanks, 2015).

The grading rubrics also promote a focus on language. Texts which fail in the evidence component are noted to 'rarely distinguish between the writer's ideas and source ideas and quotes, paraphrases and summaries are not clearly and consistently introduced, integrated and analysed to support arguments'. In the style component, weak texts are those where 'language significantly interferes with communication of ideas with frequent grammar and/or punctuation errors, inconsistent points of view, significant problems with syntax, diction and word choice'.

This lack of language focus is not only prevalent at USF but is a wider FYC issue. Jeffery and Wilcox (2013) highlight that for US high school students, their National Assessment of Educational Progress exam requires them to write opinion-based essays about large-scale topics where their evidence is personal. Similarly, international university entrants who are second language writers are often asked to discuss the extent to which they agree/disagree with a particular statement (Moore & Morton, 2005).

Considering these shortcomings, FYC researchers have started to adopt more corpus-based approaches to researching language use by FYC writers (e.g., Aull, 2017, 2019; Eckstein & Ferris, 2018). For example, Aull (2017) examines the variation in language use across FYC genres with a corpus of USF texts by looking at differences in the keywords that each genre's texts contain.

While these studies present a picture of student language use on FYC programmes, there are several unexplored paths. There are still unanswered questions as to how writers use language and, importantly, how raters view this language use when judging project tasks. Therefore, the work in this Element aims to further highlight the role language plays in first-year writing by examining the relationship collocation has with the construct of writing quality. In doing so, several contextual and learner variables that relate to the writing task and the language status of the writer are also considered to appreciate how these factors may also influence writing quality score variation.

3 Review of Collocation-Writing Quality Studies

3.1 Overview of Section

This section reviews relevant literature to set out the research landscape of collocation-grade studies. In doing so, we create a space for our work to contribute to filling identified gaps and addressing issues we raise in this area.

3.2 Definitions of Collocation and Methods of Identification

The frequency-based approach to defining and identifying collocations is influenced by two guiding principles: recurrence and co-occurrence. Recurrence is the repetition of the same word combination by a language user or a group of users (Ellis, 2008). It can be captured by looking at frequencies of word pairings in corpus data (Evert, 2004). Co-occurrence is an attraction between two words, captured by their appearance together more often than their individual frequencies would predict (Evert, 2004). As Evert (2009) notes, the mere repetition of a word pair is not a sufficient indicator of a strong attraction between the words; a pair may be frequent without there being a strong attraction between the individual words. This is seen, for example, when a combination is frequent, but its component words are able to take many other partners. Schmitt and Schmitt (2020) illustrate that the word '*the*' co-occurs with almost every non-proper noun and thus does not have strong attraction to other words. Schmitt and Schmitt (2020, p. 5) also explain that some words co-occur with only a small number of other words. The word '*blonde*', for example, occurs almost exclusively with '*hair*' and a few other nouns such as '*woman*' or '*lady*'. We produce '*blonde hair*', '*blonde woman*', or '*blonde lady*' but never '*blonde wallpaper*' or '*blonde paint*' (italics in authors' original), although these latter combinations are syntactically and semantically possible.

Firth (1968) discusses attraction as relating to the 'mutual expectancy' of words, while Sinclair (1991) draws on the 'mutual choice' that words seem to be subject to. These ideas of predictability and chance were also earlier captured in the work of Osgood (1952):

> If in the past experience of the source, events A and B ... have occurred together, the subsequent occurrence of one of them should be a condition facilitating the occurrence of the other: the writing or speaking of one should tend to call forth thinking about and hence producing the other.
>
> (Osgood, 1952, pp. 54–5)

Seretan (2011) ties these notions of frequency and predictability to key principles of statistics, namely: tendency and typicality. She highlights how scholars have defined a collocation as a typical, specific, and characteristic combination of words which are arbitrary, recurrent word combinations. Bringing these views together, collocations therefore comprise two or more words that appear near each other in a recurrent manner, and that co-occur more often than could be explained by random chance.

Traditional methods of capturing collocation have been termed positional as they operate under a span approach. This span is set by the researcher or by the software they are using and has been classically stated as four words to the left or right of the search word. However, this span of four words has been challenged (e.g., Smadja (1993), who uses five words). In many second language studies, it has been set at one or two words to only capture adjacent pairs (e.g., Bestgen, 2017; Bestgen & Granger, 2014; Granger & Bestgen, 2014). Seretan (2011) recognises the dangers of a span approach because it may capture syntactic noise – that is, word pairs which have no syntactic relationship. This is shown in example [1], whereby a span approach might capture 'human rights', and 'human rights organisations' as pairings but also the unrelated 'human organisations'.

[1]   Human rights organisations

Seretan (2011) also notes that the span approach would fail to capture pairs if they fell outside the span boundary, as with 'problem solved' in example [2]:

[2]   The **problem** is therefore clearly a deeply rooted one and cannot be **solved** without concerted action by all parties.

Recognising these limitations, others have recommended capturing syntactically related combinations by using automated tools such as the Stanford parser (Manning et al., 2014). These parsers can capture multiple dependencies such as adjectives pre-modifying a common noun, adverbs modifying an adjective. These methods have the advantage of retrieving combinations efficiently. However, their accuracy with learner writing has only recently started to be documented, so researchers need to exercise caution in their use (e.g., see Durrant & Brenchley, 2021; Huang et al., 2018; and the special issue on working with learner data edited by Kyle (2021)).

The sub-sections that follow outline the vast array of association measures that have been used to capture the property of co-occurrence, but importantly have not been acknowledged much in first or second language writing studies. A full discussion of each measure's respective formula is beyond the scope of this Element; however, full details of the formulas are provided in the supplementary material at: https://leemccallum.net/resources

3.2.1 Measures of Significance and Measures of Association Strength

Association measures can be divided into two main groups, each with its own sub-group: significance-testing measures, and strength of association measures. This distinction overlaps strongly with that between recurrence and co-occurrence discussed in the previous section, with significance-testing measures emphasising combinations that frequently recur, while strength of association measures emphasise combinations that co-occur with high levels of exclusivity.

Significance-testing measures have been divided into different sub-groups which use frequency information sometimes similarly and sometimes markedly differently. Literature (e.g., Evert, 2004; Pecina, 2005, 2010) has presented groupings labelled *likelihood*, *exact hypothesis*, and *asymptotic measures*. These measures have some similarities, but they treat the given frequency information slightly differently from a theoretical perspective and so can allocate high values to certain word combinations over others. For example, Evert's (2004) discussion of five likelihood measures (multinomial likelihood, hypergeometric likelihood, binomial likelihood, Poisson likelihood, and Poisson-Stirling) draws attention to the fact that these are in fact manipulations of each other. They build on previous measures to phase out mathematical bias by paying attention to skewed frequencies, and in doing so they draw attention to different types of word combinations.

As noted in Section 1, the t-score has emerged as a popular representative of significance measures. In language learning studies, high-scoring t-score combinations tend to include word pairings which are frequently used across different genres, disciplines, and domains. For example, in their study of intermediate and advanced CEFR (Common European Framework of Reference) second language writing, Granger and Bestgen (2014) found that pairings such as 'prime minister' (t-score: 97.2), 'other hand' (t-score: 73.9), 'long time' (t-score: 64.2), 'other people' (t-score: 61.5), 'young people' (t-score: 59.5), 'other words' (t-score:56.9), 'wide range' (52.3), and 'little bit' (49.9) were all amongst the highest scoring t-score combinations. There is a tradition of taking a t-score of 2 or greater to indicate that a word pairing is likely to be a collocation, probably based on a dubious analogy with t-scores of 1.96, marking the threshold for $p < 0.05$ in inferential statistics. However, there is no real basis for such a threshold in collocation research, where sample sizes are enormous and the assumptions on which parametric statistics are based are not usually met. Like other association measures, t-scores are best seen as a method for ranking collocations, rather than for marking sharp cut-offs between collocations and non-collocations.

Similarly, measures in the strength of association group have also been divided into different sub-groups. These include point estimate, coefficients, information theory, and heuristic measures. Of these measures, the MI has been favoured. It taps into the strength of the association or attraction between words in the pairing and so quantifies the notion of mutual expectancy. The formula captures how much we expect to see word 2 if we see word 1. It therefore quantifies the degree of exclusivity that words in a pairing have with each other. In language studies, the MI has been found to highlight low-frequency pairings which comprise more exclusive pairings, with these pairings also used in a narrower range of genres, disciplines, and domains. For example, Granger and Bestgen (2014) found that their highest scoring MI combinations included nitrous oxide (MI: 17.4), hippocractic oath (MI:16.4), conscientious objectors (MI:15.9), juvenile delinquency (MI: 15.1), ultraviolet radiation (MI: 13.8), and conscientious objection (MI: 12.6). Like the t-score, MI has often operated on a threshold basis, with a value of ≥ 3 taken to be evidence of collocation. As with the t-score threshold, there is little basis for such a cut-off, and MI is best seen as a gradient score, ranking more versus less exclusive combinations.

It is important to note here that the measures introduced thus far are based on an understanding that words mutually attract each other in a symmetrical manner. However, later work has shown that attraction is in fact asymmetrical where either word 1 or word 2 has greater power of attraction in the combination.

3.2.2 Asymmetrical Measures

Gries (2013a) has explained that a combination is often far more important for one of its elements than for the other. In the pair *upside down*, for example, *upside* is strongly associated with *down*, but the reverse is not true. This becomes especially important in research that depends on the idea that words 'predict' each other. While the occurrence of *upside* strongly predicts the occurrence of *down*, the occurrence of *down* does not strongly predict the occurrence of *upside*.

The asymmetrical nature of attraction between words has been captured by the Delta P measure. Delta P assigns separate scores for the extent to which word 1 predicts word 2 (Delta P w2 | w1: e.g., how strongly *upside* predicts *down*) and the extent that word 2 predicts word 1 (Delta P w1| w2: e.g., how strongly *down* predicts *up*). Its values range from -1 to $+1$ (Schneider, 2020).

The narratives in the previous sub-sections highlight both the array of measures mentioned across the literature and the difficulty of coherently synthesising their use. The narrative brings to light the number of measures being mentioned but also illuminates the patchy nature of their groupings and attention. The narrative further points to some scholars focussing narrowly on a small group of measures, for example, Dunning's (1993) focus on likelihood measures while others focus on multiple measures with limited explanations between their connections and differences (e.g., Pecina, 2005, 2010). There are now many voices in the language learning community calling for a better understanding of association measures (e.g., Gablasova et al., 2017a, 2017b; Gries & Durrant, 2021; Schneider, 2020; Wiechmann, 2008). Among these voices, the fragmented nature of measure attention has been raised (e.g., Gries & Durrant, 2021), as have calls to understand the relations between measures better (e.g., Wiechmann, 2008) and for measure selection to be less arbitrary (Gablasova et al., 2017b).

We now turn to show how the use of association measures has played a key role in operationalising the construct of phraseological complexity and its relationship to student writing quality. Later, we highlight how the language learning/assessment literature has used a relatively narrow range of association measures and the implications of this.

3.3 Phraseological Complexity and Its Measurement

3.3.1 The Importance of Phraseological Complexity in Learner Writing

Phraseological complexity is a relatively new term, first coined by Paquot (2019). However, the theoretical sub-constructs it is based on have a longer history. Paquot (2019, p. 124) defines phraseological complexity 'as the range of phraseological units that surface in language production and the degree of sophistication of such units'. The sub-constructs of lexical range (also known as diversity) and sophistication have a long history in vocabulary knowledge and language complexity research. For example, this might involve knowledge of the semantic meanings a word may have and/or its syntactic patterns (Durrant et al., 2021). Researchers have often studied the diversity of vocabulary items learners have used (e.g., Kyle & Crossley, 2016). Sophistication has been operationalised in multiple ways but essentially focusses on counting the different words or structures learners use which are beyond 'everyday' struc-tures/words. This picture of 'everyday' is often built up by looking at the frequencies of the structures/words with less-frequent structures/words assumed to be more sophisticated and genre- and/or discipline-specific. Under these two constructs, there is an assumption that a learner's knowledge, shown through their produced text, is focussed on being able to vary the types of language items they use and their sophistication, with the latter bound up in ideas of using genre- and/or discipline-specific or appropriate items. However, it is worth remembering that the inferences we make between learners' use of language/show of knowledge is directly related to simply analysing what is produced in their texts. The picture we obtain is limited to what language learners choose to use, rather than demonstrating all knowledge. We can assume that what is present is not necessarily their whole repertoire of knowledge or language, it is simply the language used in the text.

The production of varied and sophisticated collocation use has important implications for understanding how the use of collocations is judged or perceived by evaluators. The development of collocation use is seen as an important marker of native language use, being accepted into academic communities and signals fluent language production (Wray, 2002). Traditionally, second language writers have been known to struggle to develop this use because of the often-arbitrary constraints of combining words as well as struggling to grasp their non-literal fixed meanings (Granger & Paquot, 2009).

These struggles often present themselves as writers produce marked combinations such as 'powerful coffee' instead of 'strong coffee' (Nesselhauf, 2005). Making and demonstrating appropriate combination choices has been shown to be well received by raters in assessment studies (e.g., Bestgen, 2017; Granger & Bestgen, 2014), with marked choices less favourably so (Granger & Bestgen, 2014). Henriksen (2013) notes that the mastery of formulaic language (such as collocation) allows writers to appear fluent and gives the impression that they can fulfil a range of communicative purposes that texts demand. At university, the use of these patterns has also been seen as a kind of expected threshold at undergraduate level of study (Ward, 2007). However, knowledge/use of collocations should not be taken for granted with first language novice writers either. Indeed, comments from Römer (2009) remind us that first language novice writers are also navigating academic terrain for the first time, while Bychkovska and Lee (2017) remind us that academic writing is not a native language for anyone.

To uncover a clear picture of learners' knowledge/use of collocation and its subsequent relationship to writing quality, several studies have made implicit and explicit reference to measuring phraseological complexity. However, the clarity of this whole picture varies given the approaches to identifying collocations, methods of analyses, and different learner and reference corpora used.

3.3.2 The Knowledge Base of Phraseological Complexity in Learner Writing

The study of phraseological complexity has a shorter yet rapidly expanding history when compared to studies of syntax or vocabulary. This history is almost entirely led by studies in second language learner writing (Durrant et al., 2021).

Scholars have largely extracted collocations using a span approach (e.g., Bestgen & Granger, 2014; Granger & Bestgen, 2014), but more recent work has started to extract syntactically related pairings via automatic parsers (e.g., Paquot, 2018, 2019). Most studies have focussed on either looking at the strength of association/significance of association between words and looked at how use of these combinations differs across proficiency levels (e.g., Bestgen, 2017; Bestgen & Granger, 2014; Garner et al., 2019, 2020; Granger & Bestgen, 2014), or also looked at the diversity of collocation use using established measures of diversity (e.g., Paquot, 2018). These studies have based their analyses on a reference corpus or another resource which is often based on native writers' use of language. The work is therefore bound up in an understanding of academic writing which advocates comparing learner writing to some form of native writing.

Under this premise, scholars have looked at learners' use of word combinations in three ways: (i) counting the proportion of attested/non-attested word combinations that are found in a learner text and the reference corpus; (ii) the proportion of attested combinations which appear five or more times in the reference corpus; (iii) mean frequency of combinations where each learner text is assigned a mean frequency score based on the average frequency of all their combinations.

Using the first method, studies have found significant positive correlations between the proportion of attested word combinations and writing quality scores (e.g., Bestgen, 2017; Bestgen & Granger, 2014; Garner et al., 2020; Kim et al., 2018; Kyle & Crossley, 2016). However, an interesting contrast to these findings has been found in the earlier work of Crossley et al. (2012), in their study of 313 Freshman argumentative essays at Mississippi State University. Using the BNC as their reference corpus, they found fewer attested forms associated with the essay quality scores. This interesting contrast highlights the nuanced picture of feature–grade relationships in that what is valued in other contexts (e.g., the later works above are L2 contexts) might not be valued in other contexts, such as the mixed composition context that Crossley et al. (2012) studied.

Using the second method, results have been more nuanced. Looking at syntactic pairings such as adjective + noun, verb + noun, adverb + adjective, and noun + noun, Granger and Bestgen (2014) found that low-frequency combinations were more common at the advanced proficiency level than at the intermediate level; however, Paquot's (2018) study of L2 postgraduate writing did not find significant differences between texts rated B2-C2 on the CEFR. Using the third method, studies found positive correlations between mean frequencies and writing quality (e.g., Garner et al., 2019; Kim et al., 2018;

Kyle & Crossley, 2016), although results have differed across writing tasks, with Kyle and Crossley (2016) finding positive correlation for independent TOEFL essays but negative correlation for integrated essays, with the latter essay type being essays which are written using two reading texts as evidence. One possible explanation for this is that in the integrated essays, students borrow words from source texts (e.g., see Kyle, 2020).

Paquot (2019) captured collocation diversity by looking at the Root Type Token Ratio (RTTR) of adjective modifying noun (amod) combinations, adverbial modifiers (advmod) combinations, and direct verb object combinations (dobj). Across second language postgraduate writing, she found no significant increase in diversity across CEFR proficiency levels. Paquot (2019) is also the only study to have looked at the range of collocations via the use of a collocation list obtained from native writing. She looked at the number of collocations in second language postgraduate writing that were found in the Academic Collocation List from Ackermann and Chen (2013) but found no significant increase across proficiency levels.

Scholars have also looked at the relationship between association measures and writing quality using threshold bands and mean association scores. Both Granger and Bestgen (2014) and Paquot (2018) use threshold bands in their studies of L2 CEFR-graded texts. They split the MI into four bands: non-collocation (MI < 3), low collocation (MI ≥ 3 and < 5), mid collocation (≥ 5 and < 7), and high collocation (MI > 7). Granger and Bestgen (2014) found that advanced writers used a significantly higher proportion of high MI collocations than intermediate writers, with the latter group using more non-collocations. No significant differences were found between low- and mid-MI threshold groups. When split for part of speech, intermediate proficiency level writers used a significantly higher proportion of low-scoring pre-modifier + noun combinations. Paquot's (2018) results are harder to bring together. She found significant increases across CEFR proficiency levels for mid-MI premodifier + noun and verb + direct object combinations and for low-MI pre-modifier + noun combinations and a significant decrease for premodifier + noun non-collocations.

A more solid picture of the relationship between association measures and writing quality has emerged when scholars have used the mean MI. L2 studies have shown a consistently positive significant relationship between mean MI scores and writing quality across different L2 contexts (Bestgen, 2017; Bestgen & Granger, 2014; Garner et al., 2020; Kim et al., 2018; Paquot, 2018, 2019). In a rare investigation of FYC projects at USF, Durrant et al. (2019) found consistently weak positive non-significant correlations between the MI and the final project grades and also the independent style grade.

Two studies used the MI^2 measure, which is said to phase out the MI's favouring of low-frequency pairings. Both Garner et al. (2019) and (2020) found a significant increase in means across CEFR proficiency levels, further strengthening the evidence base that the MI and its variations are valid correlates of writing quality.

The t-score has also been studied via threshold bands and mean scores. Granger and Bestgen (2014) divided their thresholds into non-collocations (t-score < 2), low collocations (t-score ≥ 2 and 6), mid collocations (≥ 6 and < 10), and high scoring (t-score > 10). They found that intermediate level writer used significantly more high-scoring collocations than advanced level writers. Advanced writers used more low- and mid-scoring collocations. However, intermediate writers used more non-collocations. When split for part of speech, the same trends were found but fewer were statistically significant.

Other studies have used the mean t-score and found different results to Granger and Bestgen (2014). Both Bestgen and Granger (2014) and Garner et al. (2020) found that as t-score means increased, writing quality scores increased. Durrant et al. (2019) found the opposite in that there was weak negative or no correlation between two- or three-word combinations and FYC project final and style grades. These results suggest a complex picture of how the t-score may be related to writing quality.

From what has been discussed, studies have found different and sometimes opposite relationships between writing quality/development and collocations. This may be due to the different nature of the writing contexts and the methodological approaches adopted. At this point, we wish to offer critique on the methodological approaches taken in some of these studies. The use of association measure thresholds and banding raises questions about the loss of information in doing so. The often-cited premise that an MI value of ≥3 and a t-score value of ≥2 is an appropriate departure point for looking at word combinations has been the subject of increasing criticism from a variety of researchers in different disciplines. In the case of operating under the 'MI ≥ 3' captures 'interesting' combinations as opposed to <3 being 'uninteresting' (Church & Hanks, 1990), we envisage a potentially huge loss of interesting data under this cut-off point. This is particularly true when examining the production of learner combinations which may violate important language conventions and therefore be allocated low MI and/or t-scores. As already noted, we take the view that work should be based not on thresholds and cut-off points but on ranked lists of combinations, so that researchers can evaluate word combinations across the whole spectrum of scores. The t-score has also been criticised as its significance testing basis makes the measure in essence more likely to always reach significance as its values are influenced by corpus size. If the corpus used is large enough and the combination found frequently enough, it will reach more than a value of 2.0 by virtue of its reliance on corpus size and its formula make-up (Gablasova et al., 2017a). These two criticisms are acknowledged in this Element here by adopting a ranking approach over thresholds, and we also encourage use of this ranking in future studies.

It is clear here that many studies have focussed on the MI and t-score in their work with few of these studies acknowledging other alternative measures or indeed providing a concrete rationale for their focus on the MI and/or t-score. However, this is slowly changing through the use of statistical techniques which are able to tap into how association measures may be distinct from one another. Some of these statistical techniques have been shown in the learner corpus work of Kim et al. (2018), Kyle et al. (2018), Durrant et al. (2019) and Eguchi and Kyle (2020). Kim et al. (2018) found in their multidimensional factor analysis that Delta P was distinct from other association measures, while Kyle et al. (2018) found that the MI, MI^2, and Delta P were all distinct measures worth retaining for analyses in their study of TAALES 2.0 measures. In another study of TAALES, Durrant et al. (2019) also found that these association measures were distinct enough from each other to warrant retention and further analyses with their FYC data. Similarly, Eguchi and Kyle (2020) found with association measures that the Delta P, MI, and MI^2 were all distinct from each other and able to flag up different types of collocations.

Kim et al.'s (2018) multidimensional factor analysis study of the Yonsei English Learner Corpus found that directional association, measured by the Delta P, could explain 16.1 per cent of variation in writing proficiency grades and 31 per cent of variation in lexical proficiency grades, when placed in a regression model with other linguistic predictors (content word properties, bigram mutual information, bigram and trigram proportions, and word specificity). Kyle et al. (2018) found in a mixed corpus of L1 and L2 free-writing that Delta P values, taken from various sub-corpora in COCA, were able to explain 58 per cent of variation in lexical proficiency grades when modelled with other types of ngram measures and word property measures. More recently, Durrant et al. (2019) also extended the association measure range by studying Delta P alongside the MI and t-score. They found Delta P to have the strongest positive correlations with both final and style grades in FYC projects, although the reason for these results needs further unpacking. Garner et al. (2020) also extended the use of association measures beyond the MI and the t-score. They introduced the collexeme strength measure and found a significant positive correlation to writing quality across A2- B2 CEFR levels in a corpus of L2 writing produced by L1 Korean students.

It should also be highlighted here that the foundations of the MI and t-score being linked to writing quality is often limited to a sole focus on second language writing. The picture emerging via the limited use of the MI in first language school children's writing from Durrant and Brenchley (2021) is that MI scores do not increase linearly across school year groups. A degree of caution is therefore needed when considering how these results apply to other grading contexts. Findings suggest an idiosyncratic picture of how association measures are related to writing development/quality.

Importantly, the aforementioned narrative highlights a need that is addressed in this Element: the need to understand the trajectories of how the MI and the t-score fit into the association measure literature, how they are distinct from other measures, and how they can act as stand-alone informants of word association information.

A final point that we wish to make relates to the direction of this feature-writing quality work more broadly. The literature base has measured this relationship in a straightforward manner which takes the starting position that linguistic features, and in this Element's case, those of collocation, are a particularly prominent predictor of writing quality. However, this starting position overlooks the fact that what shapes writing quality judgements is complex when we consider the human judgements being made behind the quantitative score information.

We therefore take up the position in this Element that while we believe collocations have a place in understanding writing quality, we must acknowledge that multiple other variables are likely to play some role in shaping the end quantitative grade scores we have and use. The penultimate sub-sections of this section outline what kinds of variables should be considered and introduce the rationale for the use of mixed effects modelling as an appropriate way to consider these variables.

3.4 How Non-linguistic Variables May Shape Writing Quality

3.4.1 Contextual and Learner Variables

Scholars such as Barkaoui (2008) have noted the complexity involved in the grading process. Variables influencing this process include (i) the writing task, (ii) rater characteristics, and (iii) learner backgrounds. These variables introduce variation into the judgement process. This variation is either seen as a source of measurement error or as a factor worth exploring as the process of making judgements is partly standardised through using assessment rubrics which are intended to constrain individual practices (Barkaoui, 2008). In this Element, we therefore incorporate many of these variables into our work.

One contextual variable that stands out as receiving continuous attention is task (e.g., Carlson & Bridgeman, 1986; Quellmalz et al., 1982; Ruth & Murphy, 1988; Tedick, 1990). For example, in their study of a first language US school context, Quellzmalz et al. (1982) found that across 200 eleventh and twelfth grade writers' texts, raters awarded lower scores to narrative texts over expository texts. They speculate that raters therefore tend to score narratives more harshly. Their study shows that raters vary judgements according to tasks, casting doubt on the assumption that a good writer is a good writer irrespective of assignment. In L2 contexts, Carlson and Bridgeman (1986) note the fluid nature of how we understand writing quality and that it is not stagnant in light of task changes.

In different TOEFL-focussed studies, Guo et al. (2013) and Kyle and Crossley (2016) studied how lexical features across two tasks yielded different correlations with writing quality. Guo et al. (2013) studied independent and integrated source-based essays and found that many lexical diversity and sophistication measures yielded different positive or negative correlations with writing quality grade scores across the two tasks. Kyle and Crossley (2016) found similarly in their study of independent and integrated source-based essays. Taken together, these studies raise the possibility that certain tasks may introduce sources of variation into the scoring process.

A further variable of interest is the language background of the writer (e.g., see Brown, 1991; Huang & Foote, 2010). These studies present an inconclusive picture on how language background influences the allocation of writing grades by raters. In the United States, Brown (1991) looked at the degree of difference existing in the writing scores of native and international students taking composition courses at a US university. Results found no statistically significant differences between the two writers' groups scores; however, faculty did pay attention to different features of the writing, showing that although no major score differences existed, raters may have arrived at their scores from different perspectives. In contrast, the graduate level study from Huang and Foote (2010) found that L2 writers received consistently lower essay scores than their native counterparts. These studies show a mixed picture of how raters may have (un) conscious patterns of grading, depending on whether the essays are written by first or second language writers. It is worth bearing in mind that these findings have been largely obtained using small sample sizes and in a qualitative manner and therefore generalisation to other grading contexts is not possible.

3.4.2 Random Variation

The previous sections recognised the complexity of the grading process. A further consideration in building up this picture of being able to tap into score variation is the structure of the corpus itself, and how the sampling from the assessment context influences the scores.

In this respect, many corpus studies (e.g., Bestgen & Granger, 2014; Guo et al., 2013; Kyle & Crossley, 2016) have assumed the data points are independent from each other in the equation. In other words, scholars interested in measuring writing quality have assumed that the corpus and related contextual and learner variables are independent data points or independent observations (Barkaoui, 2008). A clear example of violating this independence assumption is where the same writer contributes more than one text to the corpus. The data points taken from those texts will be more similar than data points taken from texts written by different writers. Several methodologists have noted that there is a greater chance of Type 1 errors when these dependency assumptions are violated, meaning that the null hypothesis is incorrectly rejected (e.g., Hox, 2002).

This violation of independence has implications for how we understand relationships between feature-grades in FYC programmes like the one at USF. The unique assessment structure means that if modelled with monofactorial methods, we risk remaining unaware of the role that individual writers play in modelling collocation–grade relationships.

Overall, the literature review has highlighted the complexity of studying linguistic features such as collocations as well as acknowledging their role in the complex nature of the essay grading process. It allows us to pose the central question: which linguistic and non-linguistic variables may play a role in shaping the writing quality scores awarded to student essays in an FYC writing context?

Within this question, there is a need to understand which measures of collocation are appropriate for tapping into different properties of collocation that might be relevant to understanding learner writing. There is also a need to understand the complexity involved in the grading process when we consider non-linguistic variables and the potential role they might play in shaping grade scores. We therefore also pose two sub-questions which are relevant to providing a comprehensive answer to our central question:

1. How can we choose appropriate measures of collocation?
2. How can we measure and understand the potential role of different linguistic and non-linguistic variables involved in shaping writing quality scores in an appropriate way?

The sections of this Element that follow describe how we carried out our empirical work to answer these questions.

4 Methodology

4.1 Overview of the Section

The literature review in the previous section highlighted two key issues. The first concerns capturing different properties of collocation and leads us to ask: how can we choose appropriate measures of collocation? The second concerns how we can understand the complexity of what shapes writing quality scores, and leads us to ask: how can we measure the potential role of different linguistic and non-linguistic factors in an appropriate way?

This section describes the methodologies underlying the three studies we carried out to answer these two questions. The first study addressed question one. It focussed on carrying out a cluster analysis of a set of association measures to determine the extent to which they measured different properties of collocation. The second study addressed the next question. It focussed on carrying out a type of complex logistic regression for ordinal response variables. In our case, the ordinal response variable was the set of FYC writing quality grade scores. This modelling included several fixed and random effects/predictors. Linguistic predictors included the collocation measures from the cluster analysis described below and a measure of collocation diversity. Non-linguistic predictors comprised the writing task types, the language status of the student writers, and random individual raters and writers. The latter set of predictors were used to capture the complexity of the grading context as set out in Sections 2 and 3. The third study adds an additional level of understanding around what shapes writing quality scores by carrying out a qualitative analysis of the linguistic predictors to shed light on particular patterns that may explain the statistical results uncovered in the second study.

The sub-sections that follow provide details of our study and reference corpora, the rationale for our selection of predictors, and the technical methodological steps we took in each of the two studies.

4.2 The FYC Corpus and Using MICUSP as a Reference Corpus

The study corpus comes from a sample of FYC argumentative essays produced by L1 and L2 writers from USF's first-year writing programme. The study corpus comprises texts from Project 3 of ENC 1101 and Project 1 of ENC 1102 (see Section 2) because both focus on extensive essay writing, with Project 1 directly building on Project 3. Project 3 focusses on setting out and describing key arguments of different stakeholders, while Project 1 considers these key arguments and outlines how stakeholders can reach a compromise (see Section 2 for comprehensive project details).

A breakdown of the corpus is shown in Table 2.

A breakdown of the corpus in terms of grades is also provided in Tables 3 and 4. Both tables show that across the modules, there are a high number of students achieving top A grade bands (scored as 13–15 points out of a total of 15) with fewer students receiving B grades (scored as 12–10 points out of a total of 15), and fewer still only just achieving passing C grade bands (scored 9–7 points out of a total of 15).

To calculate the association measures, MICUSP (Michigan Corpus of Upper-Level Student Papers, 2009) was chosen as the reference corpus. A reference corpus is a larger corpus of language which is used as a comparison to the study corpus. In this case, a reference corpus is used to calculate the association measure values. Each dependency from the FYC 'study' corpus is looked up in MICUSP and from the frequency information in MICUSP, the association measure value is calculated. MICUSP was chosen because it contains similar tasks and topics to the tasks FYC writers would be expected to complete in their academic studies after completing the FYC programme. These tasks included argumentative writing like the FYC module tasks but also included literature reviews, lab reports, critical summaries of texts, and empirical research reports. Tasks were completed by L1 and L2 writers across multiple years of study and disciplines, including biology, education, economics, history, and engineering. Topics vary but include 'fruit fly experiments' and 'standardised testing in education'. The use of the corpus complied with the MICUSP Fair Use Statement (Michigan Corpus of Upper-Level Student Papers, 2009), and the formatted texts that were used to compute association measures were solely based on anonymised metadata.

Genre types were decided by two raters (Römer & O'Donnell, 2011). Forty-four per cent of texts were reports, 22 per cent of texts were argumentative writing, 17 per cent were research papers, 7 per cent were critiques, 6 per cent were proposals, 3 per cent were response papers, and 1 per cent was creative writing. A second reason for choosing MICUSP related to its size, with the corpus itself representing one of the largest corpora of student writing across multiple levels of study (undergraduate and graduate), disciplinary subject, and language backgrounds (in alignment with the study corpus), MICUSP also includes non-native student writers (e.g., Arabic, Chinese, and Spanish L1 speakers). The access to 2.8 million words of student writing contained within MICUSP was also a draw in choosing a reference corpus as it is a valid representative of authentic student writing which could act as a target for the first-year writers in this Element.

However, no corpus construction follows a smooth path, and a caveat worth mentioning here relates to control of ensuring papers were upper-level grades.

Table 2 Corpus make-up

Module	Project	Number of Texts		Words per L1 Texts			Words per L2 Texts		
		L1	L2	Mean	Min	Max	Mean	Min	Max
1101	3	262	104	1,082	615	2,279	1,100	655	1,849
1102	1	404	109	1,237	529	2,457	1,251	784	1,951

Table 3 ENC 1101 grade breakdown

	ENC 1101				
Grades	Numerical Score	# L1 Texts	# L2 Texts	Total Texts per Grade	(%) of Total Texts
A+	15	24	21	45	12.30
A	14	34	12	46	12.57
A–	13	62	26	88	24.04
B+	12	46	14	60	16.39
B	11	36	9	45	12.30
B–	10	27	11	38	10.38
C+	9	17	5	22	6.01
C	8	10	0	10	3.28
C–	7	8	4	12	2.73

Note: (# = number), % = percentage

Table 4 ENC 1102 grade breakdown

	ENC 1102				
Grades	Numerical Score	# L1 Texts	# L2 Texts	Total Texts per Grade	(%) of Total Texts
A+	15	53	19	72	14.04
A	14	63	19	82	15.98
A–	13	84	14	98	19.10
B+	12	59	13	72	14.04
B	11	56	20	76	14.81
B–	10	32	12	44	8.58
C+	9	21	6	27	5.26
C	8	15	5	20	3.90
C–	7	20	2	22	4.29

Note: (# = number), % = percentage

Summarising the creation of MICUSP, Römer and O'Donnell (2011) note that they largely depended on the student's assertion that their voluntary submission to the corpus had received an A– or A grade from their instructor. Although, Römer and O'Donnell request the name of the instructor, it is not documented how many texts were verified by asking the instructor for confirmation of grade, and it is also not elaborated in their summary or on the MICUSP repository, how writing grades were decided, according to writing rubric measures. This is a caveat worth bearing in mind when using MICUSP.

Table 5 MICUSP corpus make-up

Academic Subject	Sample Topics
Biology	• Fruit fly experiments
Economics	• The economic recession
	• Economics of the illicit drug market
Education	• The No Child Left Behind Act
	• Standardised testing
Civil and environmental engineering	• The use of reinforced concrete shear walls in steel framed buildings
	• International law and environmental policy
History	• New social history
	• Sex education in East and West Germany
Industrial and operational engineering	• Developing a student transport plan in Downtown Detroit
	• External analysis of the National Society of Black engineers

A breakdown of the MICUSP corpus in terms of academic subjects and topics is provided across Tables 5 and 6.

4.3 Identifying and Checking Dependencies

FYC and MICUSP texts were cleaned up by removing titles, reference lists, and references to figures and mathematical formulas to preserve student-produced language and avoid third-party tables, charts, graphs, and formulas. Both corpora were lemmatised and POS (part of speech) tagged and parsed using the Stanford Core NLP annotators (Manning et al., 2014) (version 3.9.2) through the command line. Table 7 shows these procedures. Scripts One and Two were originally written by the second author as part of the work carried out in Durrant et al. (2019), while Scripts Three and Four were written as part of the work carried out in Durrant and Brenchley (2021).

A sample of the parsed output is provided in Table 8. This table can be understood as showing the sentence ID (sentence number in the text), the word number, word in its original form, the lemma of that word, its part of speech (POS) as tagged under the Penn Treebank system (Marcus et al., 1993), the word number being depended on (dep_on), and the dependency. In this Element, we based our work on the following five dependency types in their lemma forms:

Table 6 MICUSP disciplines and writer backgrounds

Academic Division	Academic Discipline	# Texts (*n* = 829)	# Words (2,367,652)	# L1 Writers (*n* = 681)	# L2 Writers (*n* = 148)
Humanities and arts (*n* = 223)	English (ENG)	98	253,580	90	8
	History and classical studies (HIS_CLS)	40	146,820	38	2
	Linguistics (LIN)	41	142,820	34	7
	Philosophy (PHI)	44	124,500	39	5
Social sciences (*n* = 309)	Economics (ECO)	25	66,320	16	9
	Education (EDU)	46	137,502	42	4
	Political science (POL)	62	196,543	53	9
	Psychology (PSY)	104	290,310	81	23
	Sociology (SOC)	72	205,049	51	21
Biological and health sciences (*n* = 171)	Biology (BIO)	67	148,433	57	10
	Natural Resources (NRE)	62	154,348	57	5
	Nursing (NUR)	42	143,694	30	12
Physical sciences (*n* = 126)	Civil and environmental engineering (CEE)	31	85,952	25	6
	Industrial and operations engineering (IOE)	42	119,271	27	15
	Mechanical engineering (MEC)	32	110,675	22	10
	Physics (PHY)	21	41,835	19	2

Note: The 2,367,652 words are after text clean-up of the original texts.

Table 7 Text pre-analysis workflow

Steps	Tools	Corpora Used	R Script
Lemmatisation Part of speech (POS) tagging Parsing	Stanford Core NLP annotators	FYC corpus MICUSP	Parsing script (Script One)
Tidy up parsing format	R programming	FYC corpus MICUSP	Tidy up parse script (Script Two)
Extraction of dependencies	R programming	FYC corpus MICUSP	Extraction script (Script Three)
Manual parser check	Manual annotation	FYC corpus	No script used
Compute corpus-based frequencies	R programming	FYC corpus MICUSP	Frequencies script (Script Four)

- Adjectives with a modifying dependency (amod) on a common noun (e.g., 'serious disease')
- Adverbs with a modifying dependency on an adjective (advmod) (e.g., 'almost impossible')
- Adverbs with a modifying dependency on a verb (advmod) (e.g., 'usually tend')
- Common nouns with a subject dependency on a verb (nsubj) (e.g., 'show charisma')
- Common nouns with a direct object dependency on a verb (dobj) (e.g., 'feel anxiety').

Dependencies were extracted using 'Script Three'. This script read through each text and extracted amod, advmod, nsubj, and dobj dependencies through a function labelled 'dep.pairs'. Taking amod dependencies as an example, the function searched for rows that contained 'JJ' (adjective) in the POS column, a 'amod' tag in the dep column, and a 'dep_on' value that attaches or points to a word with 'NN' (common noun) in the POS column. The function then recorded the dependent adjective and the noun it depends on. The same procedure was used for extracting nsubj, advmod, and dobj dependencies.

Since the Stanford parser has traditionally been trained from the Penn Treebank (Marcus et al., 1993), which contains sentences from the *Wall Street Journal*, the accuracy of parsing often non-standard learner English had to be determined to ensure that the output from the parser actually contained

Table 8 Sample parser output

Sentence ID	Word_Number	Word	Lemma	POS	Dep_on	Dep
1	1	Wearing	Wear	VBG	7	csubj
1	2	good	good	JJ	3	amod
1	3	clothes	clothes	NNS	1	dobj
1	4	is	be	VBZ	7	cop
1	5	the	the	DT	7	det
1	6	best	best	JJS	7	amod
1	7	way	way	NN	0	root
1	8	to	to	TO	9	mark
1	9	show	show	VB	7	acl
1	10	charisma	charisma	NN	9	dobj
1	11	and	and	CC	9	cc
1	12	leave	leave	VB	9	conj
1	13	a	a	DT	15	det
1	14	good	good	JJ	15	amod
1	15	impression	impression	NN	12	dobj
1	16	to	to	TO	17	case
1	17	others	other	NNS	12	nmod
1	18	.	.	.	7	punct

dependency combinations. For this check, the first author worked with a second annotator to check the POS tagging and dependency accuracy. Both annotators followed the original annotation guidelines from Marcus et al. (1993) and De Marneffe and Manning (2008). Ten texts per grade level, which amounted to over 20 per cent of the total corpus (180 of 879 texts) were chosen for the check. The first author checked 10 per cent of the 180 texts (i.e., 18 texts) by recording the POS tags and then the dependency pairs. The second annotator coded the same eighteen texts and recordings between the two annotators were compared. Agreement was high for POS tags (92 per cent) and dependencies (86 per cent), and so the first author then coded the remaining 162 texts independently. This coding was then compared with the Stanford output.

Table 9 shows the parser performance in terms of precision and recall across grade level, rounded to the nearest percentage. The table also shows that the greatest discrepancies arise from adverb modifying syntactic types. The relatively low recall scores mean that the parser was unable to capture many true adverb dependencies, and so this dependency type was not considered further in the study. These low results may be due to the fact the parser is dealing with learner English, or it might be task or feature dependent. For example, in two recent studies by Kyle et al. (2021) on verb-argument constructions and Picoral et al. (2021) on different types of phrasal and clausal structures, accuracy varied. In the former study, 80 per cent accuracy was reported and, in the latter, although higher accuracy was reported, task was seen as a potential source of variation/inaccuracy.

The other dependency findings corroborate similar checks on different structures from Berzak et al. (2016), who reported 88.07 per cent accuracy with sentences from the Cambridge Learner Corpus. Durrant and Brenchley (2021) also reported that parser precision averaged 80 per cent and recall averaged 85 per cent for amod dependencies, while for dobj dependencies, precision averaged 76 per cent and recall averaged 24 per cent with texts written by English school children. Similarly, high rates of precision and recall were also found in Kyle and Eguchi (2021), who reported an average accuracy rate for noun–adjective dependencies of 96.9 per cent, verb–adverb dependencies had an accuracy rate of 98.6 per cent, verb–direct object dependencies of 96 per cent, and verb–subject 95.4 per cent. Table 9 also shows that second language scores were consistently lower than first language scores. Although not studied further in this Element, there is evidence that learner errors have some relationship to parser errors (e.g., Huang et al., 2018), and so the premise that second language writing is often more grammatically erroneous than first language writing may be explored to provide a justification for the findings here. Equally, it should be highlighted that these results and cautions are also not

Table 9 Parser accuracy across dependency types (n = 180 texts)

Module	Writer Group	Amod				Adv mod with Adjective or Verb				Nouns with Subject Dependency on a Verb (nsubj)				Nouns with an Object Dependency on a Verb (dobj)			
		N	Recall	Precision	F1	N	Recall	Precision	F1	N	Recall	Precision	F1	N	Recall	Precision	F1
ENC 1101	L1	1,654	88%	83%	85%	897	22%	79%	34%	1,267	88%	83%	85%	608	54%	82%	65%
	L2	1,501	83%	77%	80%	711	18%	75%	29%	1,157	85%	82%	85%	493	48%	76%	59%
ENC 1102	L1	1,847	85%	80%	82%	945	24%	77%	37%	1,562	86%	84%	85%	841	42%	88%	57%
	L2	1,830	81%	76%	78%	890	19%	76%	30%	1,471	80%	82%	81%	803	36%	77%	49%
Average across all texts		**1,708**	**84%**	**79%**	**81%**	**861**	**21%**	**77%**	**42%**	**1,364**	**85%**	**83%**	**84%**	**686**	**45%**	**81%**	**58%**

limited to the domain of learner corpus research or indeed the Stanford parser. Kyle (2021) has also recently drawn attention to the fact that since parsing is dependent on prior annotation processes (tokenisation, POS tagging), there is a need to be aware that errors in these prior processes mean that the errors will also impact on the later parsing as the parser draws on these processes to carry out parsing the texts.

During this accuracy check, there were several tags and dependencies that we questioned. These often related to mistagging of individual words and therefore casting doubt on the dependencies. Examples of mistagging are shown in examples [3]–[5]. Examples [3]–[5] show inaccurate tagging with sentence [3] illustrating how the original 'JJ' tag for 'individual' should be 'NN'; sentence [4] illustrating how the original 'NNS' tag for 'states' should be a verb ('VBZ': third person singular present); and sentence [5] illustrating how the original 'NN' tag for 'addresses' should be a verb ('VBZ'):

[3]   'Adolescents may look at an **individual** and wonder why it is they themselves cannot have the life the individuals on social media have'.

[4]   'The 14th Amendment in the United States constitution **states** that anybody who is born within the borders of the United States, has the right to become an American citizen'.

[5]   'An article called the Role of Communication Technology in Adolescents Relationships and Identity Development **addresses** that on Facebook triggers states of envy and resentment in many'.

The examples in Tables 10 and 11 show the relationship between mistagging and inaccurate dependencies; in Table 10, 'committed' was tagged as an adjective 'JJ' (instead of 'VBD') and parsed incorrectly as an amod dependency. In Table 11, we see a similar issue with tagging of 'switching', which has been tagged as 'NN' (singular noun or mass noun) instead of 'VBG' (verb gerund).

4.4 The Measures Used

The rationale for choosing association measures was based on examining measures across the groupings identified in key computational work by Evert (2004), Pecina (2005, 2010) and Seretan (2011) as well as language learning studies showing differential patterns between different association measure types (e.g., Bestgen, 2017; Bestgen & Granger, 2014; Durrant & Schmitt, 2009; Gablasova et al., 2017a; Paquot, 2018, 2019). In choosing a set of association measures, we opted for measures which were already in use across different studies but also chose to include computationally simple and therefore

Table 10 Parsed output (amod)

Sentence ID	Word #	Word	Lemma	POS	Dep_on	Stanford Output
35	1	He	He	PRP	4	nsubj
35	2	too	too	RB	3	advmod
35	3	**committed**	**committed**	**JJ**	**4**	**amod**
35	4	**suicide**	**suicide**	**NN**	**0**	**root**
35	5	but	but	CC	4	cc
35	6	this	this	DT	7	det
35	7	time	time	NN	10	nmod:tmod
35	8	it	it	PRP	10	nsubj
35	9	was	be	VBD	10	cop
35	10	decades	decade	NNS	4	conj
35	11	after	after	IN	13	mark
35	12	he	he	PRP	13	nsubj
35	13	received	receive	VBD	10	advcl
35	14	his	he	PRP$	16	nmod:poss
35	15	last	last	JJ	16	amod
35	16	concussion	concussion	NN	13	dobj
35	17	.	.	.	4	punct

Table 11 Parsed output (nsubj)

Sentence ID	Word #	Word	Lemma	POS	Dep_on	Stanford Output
46	1	**Switching**	Switching	NN	5	**nsubj**
46	2	to	to	TO	3	case
46	3	vegetarianism	vegetarianism	NN	1	nmod
46	4	can	can	MD	5	aux
46	5	save	save	VB	0	root
46	6	not	not	RB	7	neg
46	7	only	only	RB	9	cc:preconj
46	8	the	the	DT	9	det
46	9	environment	environment	NN	5	dobj
46	10	but	but	CC	9	cc
46	11	also	also	RB	13	advmod
46	12	can	can	MD	13	aux
46	13	help	help	VB	9	conj
46	14	improve	improve	VB	13	ccomp
46	15	health	health	NN	14	dobj
46	16	.	.	.	5	punct

more easily comparable measures which focussed on the basic idea of using contingency tables. This meant that we did not opt to use those measures labelled *context measures* in Pecina (2005, 2010) as these involved many complex mathematical calculations and were also measures which had no background in the literature we drew upon to guide our work. We wanted to use measures that would have some familiarity to as many potential readers as possible. Table 12 shows the final set of forty-seven association measures. The formulae for these forty-seven measures can be found in the supplementary materials on https://leemccallum.net/resources. The association measure values were calculated by extending the calculator developed by Durrant (2020), where each column contained one association measure and each row contained

Table 12 Association measures for the cluster analysis

Measure	Measure
Poisson-Stirling Log Measure	Yulle's Q
T-Score	Driver-Kroeber
Z-Score	Fifth Sokal Sneath
Chi-squared test	Pearson
Loglikelihood ratio	Baroni-Urbani
Squared loglikelihood ratio	Braun-Blanquet
MI	Simpson
Relative risk	Michael
Dice coefficient	Mountford
Mutual expectation	Fager
Jaccard	Unigram subtuples
Geometric mean	U cost
Minimum sensitivity	S cost
Odds ratio	R cost
Odds ratio disc	T combined cost
Russel-Rao	Normalised expectation
Sokal-Michner	MI^3
Rogers-Tanimoto	Log frequency-based mutual dependency
Hamann	Mutual dependency
Third-Sokal Sneath	salience
First Kulczynsky	Delta P w2 | w1
Second Sokal Sneath	Delta P w1 | w2
Second Kulczynsky	
Fourth Sokal Sneath	
Yulle's ω	

a dependency, so across each row we could simply obtain an entry for each of the forty-seven association measures.

4.5 The Cluster Analysis Rationale and Procedures

To engage with the first question ('How can we choose appropriate measures of collocation?') we carried out a cluster analysis to illuminate measures which could tell us different types of information about collocation properties.

As a type of statistical analysis, cluster analysis is used to group similar cases (or variables in our study) together. In our study, what is being grouped together is the association measures. They are grouped together according to how similarly they assign an association score to the dependency pairs. This is a similar procedure to factor analysis (both exploratory and confirmatory) in the sense that all three group similar cases/variables together according to their similar properties (e.g., assigning similar values to items). Factor analysis was used in some of the studies mentioned in Section 3 in discussing how association measures may be tapping into different or similar properties of collocation (e.g., see Durrant et al., 2019; Kim et al., 2018; Kyle et al., 2018). However, the added benefit of choosing to tap into these potential similar and distinct groupings via a cluster analysis is that the technique visualises these groupings via a related heatmap of correlations and dendrogram. Both visualisations can be used alongside the numerical correlation data to inform our understandings of association measures.

The cluster analysis was based on dependencies that appeared five or more times in the reference corpus so as to ensure association measure calculations were reliable (e.g., see Paquot, 2018, 2019). Table 13 shows those below threshold and absent dependencies which were not included in the cluster analysis and the total number of types that were included. Below threshold dependencies were dependencies appearing fewer than five times in MICUSP. Absent dependencies were those not found in MICUSP at all. The large percentage of absent and below threshold combinations are most likely to be because MICUSP is still a relatively small corpus for retrieving multi-word

Table 13 FYC dependency types included in the cluster analysis

Dependency Type	# Types	Below Threshold Types (%)	Absent Types (%)	# Types in Analyses
amod	11,982	23	38	4,673
nsubj	3,903	28	46	1,054
dobj	9,868	43	33	2,368

combinations, the latter being somewhat less frequent than individual words, even in large general corpora.

A snapshot of the most frequently occurring dependencies in the FYC corpus and their status in MICUSP is presented at https://leemccallum.net/resources

Hierarchical clustering was used to show the relations between the association measures as determined by the data rather than a predetermined theory from the literature (Field et al., 2012). Hierarchical cluster analysis was chosen because the analysis aimed to use the clustering as an exploratory method to show connections between measures, emerging from the data itself rather than any predetermining theory from the literature or the researcher (Field et al., 2012). This contrasts to non-hierarchical clustering where the researcher may predetermine the number of desired clusters (Levshina, 2015). Crawley (2013, p. 819) explains: 'The idea behind hierarchical cluster analysis is to show which of a (potentially large) set of samples are most similar to one another, and to group these similar samples in the same limb of a tree. Groups of samples that are distinctly different are placed in other limbs'. This similarity is decided based on the distance between two samples. In this study of clustering variables, the distance is the distance between pairs of association measures.

To check the validity of the clustering solution, we checked the Average Silhouette Width (ASW), which represents how well-formed the clusters are and indicates how confident we can be in the clustering solution (Levshina, 2015). The statistic ranges from –1 to 1, with –1 indicating no clustering in the data and 1 indicating perfect separation of all clusters (Brock et al., 2008). Levshina (2015) advises that an ASW value <0.2 signals a lack of substantial cluster structure in the data. This validity check is discussed in Section 5.

These decisions helped determine the different clusters in the cluster analysis solution and helped us determine which measures to retain and which to discard, thus developing an understanding of how we can distinguish between association measures which tap into similar/different collocation properties.

4.6 The Statistical Modelling Rationale and Procedures

To engage with the second question: 'how can we measure and understand the potential role of different linguistic and non-linguistic variables in an appropriate way?', we created an ordinal type of mixed effects model. In other words, the model was used to measure the role different variables played in shaping score variations in the FYC corpus. This aligns with comments from Loerts et al. (2020), who view essay grades as ordinal variables. The mixed model was a cumulative links model which treats the dependent variable ('Final_Grade') as ordinal and represents the effect of the independent variable on the dependent variable as logit odds, in a similar manner to Haberman and Sinharay (2010). These odds represent the chance of the independent variable having an effect on the dependent variable (O'Connell, 2006). In line with established cumulative links modelling practices, these logit odds were transformed into more intuitive odds ratios (Winter, 2020).

To measure diversity, we followed Paquot (2019) and more recent studies (e.g., Jiang et al., 2021) and calculated the RTTR for each dependency type: amod, nsubj, and dobj. The ratio was calculated by dividing the number of types by the square root of the number of tokens. We choose the RTTR due to its consistent use in the literature, for example see its continued use over time in vocabulary studies (e.g., Bulté & Housen, 2014; Daller et al., 2013; Hou et al., 2016; Kim, 2014; Llanes et al., 2018; Lorenzo & Rodríguez, 2014; Treffers-Daller et al., 2018; Verspoor et al., 2017) as well as the aforementioned phraseological studies. The measure itself is also simple to calculate and easily interpreted: the higher the value, the more diverse the text is taken to be. However, it should be noted that like most other diversity measures, the RTTR is influenced by text length effects and this caveat should be remembered when using this measure of diversity.

First, the linguistic predictors of the RTTR and association measures were centred and standardised following procedures from Gries (2013b). These procedures allow variables to operate on a scale of standard units, thus making variables comparable. Centring and standardisation procedures are also recommended to avoid possible model convergence issues (Winter, 2020).

The fixed effects of task and language status were coded as categorical variables with two levels (1 and 2), with the variable names 'task 1' and 'task 2' and 'Language_status1' and 'Language_status2' with Language_status1 = first language (native) speaker of English and 'Language_status2' = second language (non-native) speaker of English. In the model, the algorithm in R chooses one of these levels to act as a reference level and uses this reference level as a comparison with the other levels. The choice of reference level is often alphabetical or the first numerical level (Levshina, 2015). In the model output, the reference level will not be shown, but the level compared to it will be (e.g., see Liu, 2016; Winter, 2020, p. 184). This means that for the model output in Figure 4, 'Language_status1' (native speaker) is the reference level with the model output showing the significant result for 'Language_status2' (non-native speaker).

All models were created in R (Version 3.6.3) (R Core Development Team, 2014) using the ordinal package (Christensen, 2019). The mixed effects model was created by following the three-stage process set out by Gries (2015). Stage one involved generating a maximal fixed effects model. Stage two involved generating a maximal random effects model. These two stages are described in McCallum (2021). Stage three joined these two models together to create the mixed model. The fixed effects model initially included all possible fixed effects predictors. These included the association measures from the cluster analysis for each dependency type, the Root TTR for each dependency type, and the effects of task and the writers' language status. This 'full' model was then trimmed to remove non-significant predictors, with each new model compared to the previous one via the 'anova' function. The AIC (Akaike Information Criteria) values were inspected and the model with the lowest value was chosen as the most parsimonious model. The most parsimonious model was the one able to explain the most variance using the fewest number of predictors.

Stage two involved establishing the maximal random effects structure. An examination of the FYC data set indicated that individual writers contributed more than one essay to the corpus. We therefore modelled this random variation in line with other modelling works such as Paquot (2019) and Durrant and Brenchley (2021).

To also answer the second question, we qualitatively inspected texts containing high- and low-scoring association measures and diversity scores in the FYC corpus. This analysis is presented in Section 7.

5 Study One: The Cluster Analysis

5.1 Overview of Section

The cluster analysis in this section answers the first question that we engage with: 'how can we choose appropriate measures of collocation?' The cluster analysis essentially groups together similar association measures in the sense that they assign similar values to the same dependency pair. In doing so, it highlights similar pairs and therefore larger clusters of measures while at the same time illuminating those association measures which are dissimilar and clearly tapping into different collocation properties.

This section presents the results of the cluster analysis. These results are interpreted using different sources of information. Key to this interpretation is the visual understanding of the measures we obtain from the cluster dendrogram itself (see Figure 1), in addition to the original heatmap correlations which were used to generate the clustering. These two visuals allow us to see the specific robust nature of the clustering and also put this clustering into perspective by considering how individual pairs of measures within and between clusters are correlated. The information here is therefore systematic and visual rather than making connections between measures through solely inspecting lists ranked association measure scores as Brezina (2018) and others have presented. A third source of information that we refer to is the theoretical criteria/guidance offered by Gablasova et al. (2017a). Gablasova et al. (2017a) present several theoretical criteria that researchers should consider for measure selection. These criteria relate to (i) the mathematical computation of the measure, (ii) the scale the measure operates on, and (iii) each measure's practical effect in how its formula is able to illuminate or downgrade particular word combinations.

5.2 The Clustering and Its Validation

The dendrogram in Figure 1 visually represents the (dis)similarity amongst association measures. It has been rotated 90 degrees to aid readability. The x-axis represents the linkage distance between the objects. This height symbolises the differences between the measures where the greater the height, the bigger the difference between variables in the cluster analysis. This figure also illuminates several 'branches' that connect the association measures that are being clustered. These branches vary in length, and the longer in length, the greater the difference between the measures (Gries, 2013b). The y-axis shows the association measures that are clustered together. As Wiechmann (2008) recognises, the interpretation of a dendrogram is often influenced by the researcher's subjective judgement, and so the discussion has a degree of subjectivity from our own interpretation of the clustering.

5.2.1 Determining the Number of Clusters

The dendrogram visually supports three to six large clusters with several sub-clusters also apparent. To check the clustering's internal validity, we calculated the ASW which represents how well-formed the clusters are and indicates how confident we can be in the clustering solution (Levshina, 2015). This was calculated with the silhouette function in the cluster package (Maechler et al., 2015). The statistic ranges from -1 to $+1$, with -1 indicating no clustering in the data and $+1$ indicating perfect separation of all clusters (Brock et al., 2008). Levshina (2015) advises that an ASW value <0.2 signals a lack of substantial cluster structure in the data. The ASW statistic for the three to six clusters is presented in Table 14.

The ASW values suggest greatest support for five clusters, with the lower ASW value for six clusters indicating less stability. Figure 2 highlights these five clusters. It has been rotated 90 degrees to aid readability.

Table 14 Average silhouette width

Cluster	3	4	5	6
ASW Values	0.323	0.328	0.341	0.333

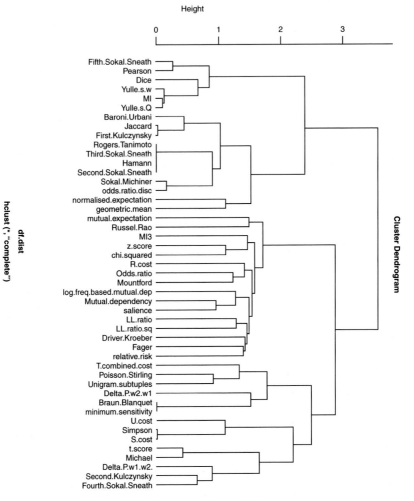

Figure 1 Dendrogram of association measures

5.3 Measure Retention

A valid consideration in making retention decisions is a measure's history in language learning studies and the interpretability and performance of the measure with actual language data. Further to this, a key reason for the cluster analysis was to understand the place of the MI and the t-score in the literature and to uncover how different other measures are to those two measures which act as pillars representing exclusivity and frequency, as highlighted by Brezina (2018).

The dendrogram in Figure 2 presents one perspective on this. More detailed information can be gleaned from a heatmap representing the correlation matrix between all measures. This is shown in Figure 3. The strongest correlations are

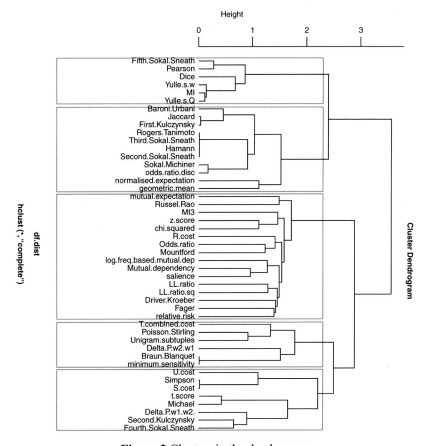

Figure 2 Clusters in the dendrogram

in red; shades of purple represent weak to approaching moderate correlations ($r = 0.30$–0.70) and white represents little correlation between measures. A downloadable visualisation of this map can be found at https://leemccallum .net/resources

5.4 Between and within Cluster Observations

To determine levels of similarity between the association measures, we can make observations both between clusters and within individual clusters in the dendrogram.

In Cluster 1, the lack of height between the MI and Yulle's ω and Yulle's Q suggests these are more similar than any of the other measures. There appears to be a small degree of difference between the Dice measure and the other cluster members because of its greater branch height. Given this high

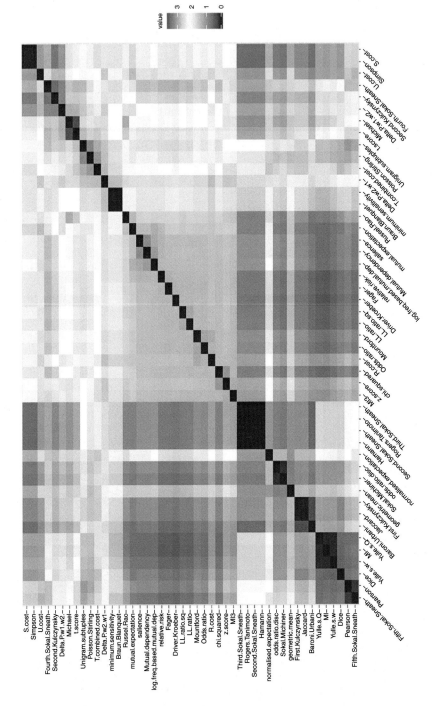

Figure 3 Heatmap showing relationships across association measures

collinearity and that we know the MI and Log Dice have been shown to tap into exclusivity, this leads to a conclusion that the measures in this cluster flag up exclusive pairings. Although when comparing the MI and Log Dice, Gablasova et al. (2017a) support the scaling of the Log Dice because compared to the MI, it has a theoretical limit. Comparative work between the MI and the Log Dice has also found that the measures are highly correlated (Öksuz et al., 2021) and when entered into a mixed effects model on collocation processing times with first and second language speakers, the Log Dice produced a better explanatory model than the MI. However, explanations around why this might be the case are in their infancy. In our study, we set out as taking both the MI and the t-score as representative association measures, seeking to learn about their relationships with other measures. Therefore, we take the MI as our starting marker and look at the relationships it has with other clusters' members. However, this first cluster, like the other clusters, serves as a reminder that analysts are faced with making pairwise choices between association measures, whereby they should choose measures that are appropriate for their study's aims.

From Cluster 2 to 5, there is a move away from exclusivity with measures sharing less correlations with the cluster of measures first represented in Cluster 1. Cluster 2 contains many measures that do not have an established connection to language learning, teaching, or assessment research. In weighing up measure retention, Figure 3's heatmap indicates strong correlations between Jaccard and First Kulczynsky; and between Rogers-Tanimoto, Third Sokal Sneath, Hamann, and Second Sokal Sneath. The correlations between these measures exceed $r = 0.80$ and the measures show high collinearity with other measures in Cluster 1 (e.g., the correlation between the Third Sokal Sneath and Log Dice reaches $r \geq 0.73$). Following general statistics literature (e.g., Tabachnick & Fidell, 2014) on what constitutes collinearity ($r \geq 0.70–0.90$), the retention of all these measures would mean capturing very similar properties of collocation. The value of the cluster analysis appears clear here because it illuminates important relationships between coefficient measures that are sparsely elaborated on in the literature. This cluster also offers counterevidence to Schneider (2020), who comments that collinearity between association measures is rare because the clustering here shows high-measure collinearity. Given these observations, the measure which is most distinct from the MI in Cluster 1 is the geometric mean ($r = 0.64$) and so this measure is the measure retained for Cluster 2. The geometric mean is also a good measure for retention because although correlated with its cluster members, these correlations do not violate collinearity ($r = 0.68$).

Cluster 3's starting height and branch length indicate that these measures share less collinearity than other clusters. Many measures originate from hypothesis testing, hence a degree of correlation between them. When the correlations in the heatmap are explored, the strongest correlation exists between mutual expectation and Russel Rao ($r = 0.18$). All other measures have low to no correlation. Gries and Durrant (2021) previously noted that association measures are manipulations or regressions of each other, and while this is indeed true for much of the observations in other clusters, Cluster 3 shows measures with little correlation.

Considering the measures in Cluster 3, the most enduring measures in the language learning literature have been significance test measures. For example, the z-score, the odds ratio, and the Loglikelihood Ratio and Loglikelihood Ratio Squared (LLR^2) have all been featured in several language studies (e.g., Evert, 2009). Support for Loglikelihood measures is most consistent across the literature (e.g., Dunning, 1993; Evert, 2004, 2009; Pecina, 2005), while measures such as the odds ratio are criticised for being difficult to interpret (Evert, 2009). There is a pragmatic argument to be made that either of the Loglikelihood measures are valid retention choices, given their support in the literature (e.g., Evert, 2004); however, there is more of a tendency to favour more mathematically robust and less-bias measures that do not overinflate language data (Evert, 2004), and so the squared loglikelihood ratio seems to be the most pragmatic retained measure in Cluster 3.

In Cluster 4, there is little difference between 'Braun Blanquet' and 'Minimum Sensitivity', while the 'T Combined Cost' is distinct from other measures and 'Poisson Stirling' and 'Unigram Subtuples' have some degree of difference. The other two measures – Braun Blanquet and Minimum Sensitivity – are highly correlated ($r = 1.00$). It is also worth noting here that while the Minimum Sensitivity has gained favour in some studies by performing well in identifying collocations (e.g., Weichmann, 2008), its use has been advised with caution as its values are difficult to interpret (Gries, 2013b), its close relationship to the Braun Blanquet also means the same caveats should apply to Braun Blanquet. In contrast to the aforementioned measures, the T-combined cost and Delta P w2 | w1 appear distinct from other measures (shown by high height and lack of branch). Both measures also have lower correlations with other measures in the cluster, as indicated by the heatmap in Figure 3. Equally, in our quest to retain measures that are distinct enough from each other, referring back to the correlations between these measures in Cluster 4 and those in Cluster 1, illuminating exclusivity, the Delta P w2 | w1 is the least correlated with the MI ($r = 0.31$) when compared to the correlations between the MI and the

T-combined cost (0.44). Therefore, in Cluster 4, we retain the Delta P w2 | w1 measure.

Cluster 5 contains the following association measures: U cost, Simpson, S cost, T score, Michael, Delta P w1 | w2, Second Kulczynsky, and the Fourth Sokal Sneath. The flat height between Simpson and S cost indicates high collinearity ($r = 0.950$). These measures are also highly correlated ($r = 0.90$, $r = 0.90$) with the Second Kulczynsky and the Fourth Sokal Sneath ($r = 0.73$, $r = 0.73$). Similar high correlations are found between the t-score and Michael ($r = 0.95$).

In deciding between the t-score and Michael, the t-score has an established history in language learning and is known to illuminate high-frequency pairings that are typical across genres/disciplines (e.g., Durrant & Schmitt, 2009; Granger & Bestgen, 2014) and therefore is the measure most likely to be retained. However, both the dendrogram and the heatmap show evidence that the Delta P w1 | w2 measure is distinct enough from the t-score and all other measures as evidenced in its branch height and correlation value of $r = 0.40$ with the t-score. This means that in this last cluster we retain the Delta P and the t-score for their different properties.

To sum up across the five clusters, we have chosen measures which are distinct enough from each other to suggest that they tap into different information about collocation. The analysis of the dendrogram and heatmap lead us to retain six measures, which are mathematically distinct enough to highlight different properties of collocation: the MI, the geometric mean, the LLR^2, the Delta P w2| w1, Delta P w1|w2, and the t-score.

The cluster analysis helps reveal relationships between association measures because it visually represents various relationships between measures already mentioned in the literature and measures which have received sporadic attention. The clustering also facilitates understanding by placing commonly used measures into this visual picture to reinforce their position as being viable measure candidates that tap into different collocation properties. We can see, through the individual clusters and the within cluster relationships, that the MI, the geometric mean, Loglikelihood, t-score, and Delta P are all distinct enough to suggest they illuminate different types of word combinations. This aligns with previous findings from Durrant et al. (2019), Kim et al. (2018), and Kyle et al. (2018), who found similar distinctions, with Kyle et al. (2018) also finding that the MI^2 was also sufficiently different from the MI (as is also shown in the cluster analysis here).

This section has explained how we decided which measures to retain and which to discard. It is also important to look holistically at the cluster analysis and reflect on the methodological clustering choices made at the start of Section 4. The choice of furthest neighbour clustering was made to produce tight clusters. We can see then that we have a spectrum of clusters, with Clusters 2, 3, 4, and 5 further away from the measures and underlying principle of 'exclusivity' that Cluster 1 is clearly based upon. With reference to Clusters 4 and 5, we can see a sparse picture of clustering with these measures furthest from those in Cluster 1, but not necessarily always strongly clustered together as pairs in their respective cluster. There is evidence, then, that this clustering corroborates the theoretical work of Brezina (2018) and Evert (2004, 2009), who have referred to the properties that are flagged up by the association measures, operating along a cline or continuum. This continuum goes from exclusivity at one end to more of a focus on significance testing/raw frequency measures at the other end. The visual clustering supports this work and also highlights how the Delta P continues to be distinct from this potentially dichotomous picture, given their low correlation/cluster ties with other non-directional association measures.

CLUSTER ANALYSIS HIGHLIGHTS

- Cluster 1 contains measures which tap into the property of exclusivity.
- Other clusters move gradually away from exclusivity towards other dimensions of frequency and directionality with measures in Clusters 2–5 less correlated than the exclusivity measures in Cluster 1.
- Retention decisions were made on the basis of mathematical and visual differences between cluster and sub-cluster members by using the dendrogram and the heatmap visualisations.
- The MI, geometric mean, LLR^2, Delta P w1|w2, Delta P w2|w1, and the t-score were all retained because of their ability to illuminate exclusivity, high frequency, or directionality in word pairs.
- Cluster analysis can aid decision-making for analysts by clarifying relationships between and within clusters and sub-clusters.

---

6 Study Two: The Statistical Modelling

6.1 Overview of Section

The statistical modelling presented in this section answers the second question that we engage with: 'how can we measure and understand the potential role of different linguistic and non-linguistic variables in an appropriate way?'

This section focusses on explaining the inferences we can (and cannot) make from the mixed effects modelling results. The section works together with Section 7, which follows to illuminate important relationships between collocations and writing quality and several learner and contextual variables. These sections combined give an overall picture of collocation and writing quality relationships and remind us of the strengths and limitations that such modelling work affords us.

6.2 Mixed Model Results

This section describes how the key association measures selected in the previous section – the MI, geometric mean, LLR^2, Delta P w1|w2, Delta P w2|w1, and t-score – predicted the scores assigned to texts. An overview of the independent variable predictors in terms of effect type and also their descriptive statistics are shown in Table 15.

The mixed model, generated from the optimal fixed and random models, is shown in Figure 4.

The mixed effects model in Figure 4 and its summarised information in Tables 16 and 17 shows that nine fixed effects were significant predictors of

Table 15 Descriptive statistics for numerical predictors

Predictor	Effect Type	Min	Max	Mean	SD
Mean LLR^2 amod	Fixed	1.084	1342.43	194.771	129.421
Mean MI nsubj	Fixed	0.888	2.671	0.510	0.351
Mean Delta P w2| w1 nsubj	Fixed	−0.010	0.513	0.009	0.022
Mean t-score nsubj	Fixed	−24.285	9.916	1.169	1.956
Mean MI dobj	Fixed	−1.081	3.073	0.840	0.669
Mean Delta P w1| w2 dobj	Fixed	−0.034	0.381	0.025	0.046
Amod RTTR	Fixed	3.400	10.334	6.445	1.073
Nsubj RTTR	Fixed	3.162	10.334	6.574	1.074

Note: Mean LLR^2 amod = Mean Loglikelihood Ratio Squared for amod dependencies; Mean MI nsubj = Mean MI for nsubj dependencies; Mean Delta P w2| w1 nsubj = Mean Delta P word 1 | word 2 for nsubj dependencies; Mean MI dobj = Mean MI for dobj dependencies; Mean Delta P w1|w2 dobj = Mean Delta P word 1| word 2 for dobj dependencies; Amod RTTR = Amod Root Type Token Ratio; Nsubj RTTR = Nsubj Root Type Token Ratio.

Cumulative Link Mixed Model fitted with the Laplace approximation

formula: Final_Grade ~ 1 + Mean LLR^2 amod + Mean MI nsubj + Mean Delta P w2 I w1
nsubj + Mean t-score nsubj + Mean MI dobj + Mean Delta P w1 I w2 dobj + Amod RTTR +
Nsubj RTTR + Language_status + (1 I student_id)

data: data

link threshold	**nobs**	**logLik**	**AIC**	**niter**	**max.grad**	**cond.H**
logit flexible	879	−1781.05	3598.11	2931(5884)	1.29e−03	1.2e+02

Random effects:

Groups	Name	Variance	Std.Dev.
student_id	(Intercept)	0.3936	0.6274

Number of groups: student_id 768

Coefficients:

	Estimate	**Std. Error**	**z-value**	**Pr(>|z|)**
Mean LLR^2 amod	−0.20631	0.06652	−3.101	0.00193**
Mean MI nsubj	0.32727	0.12512	2.616	0.00890**
Mean Delta P w2 I w1 nsubj	−0.20195	0.08959	−2.254	0.02419*
Mean t-score nsubj	−0.25215	0.10363	−2.433	0.01496*
Mean MI dobj	0.20151	0.07414	2.718	0.00657**
Mean Delta P w1 I w2 dobj	−0.14847	0.07009	−2.118	0.03414*
Amod RTTR	0.19577	0.07671	2.552	0.01071*
Nsubj RTTR	0.13449	0.07493	1.795	0.07268.
Language_status2	0.37620	0.15510	2.426	0.01528*

Signif. codes: 0 '***' 0.001 '**' 0.01 '*' 0.05 '.' 0.1 ' ' 1

Threshold coefficients:

	Estimate	**Std. Error**	**z-value**
7 I 8	−3.40187	0.21170	−16.069
8 I 9	−2.70724	0.16923	−15.998
9 I 10	−2.03898	0.13796	−14.779
10 I 11	−1.32128	0.11061	−11.946
11 I 12	−0.56339	0.08933	−6.307
12 I 13	0.13469	0.08365	1.610
13 I 14	1.16511	0.10497	11.100
14 I 15	2.18146	0.14449	15.098

Figure 4 Mixed effects model with individual student as random variation

the outcome variable of 'Final_Grade': eight of these predictors were
collocation measures and the ninth predictor was 'Language_status2'. The
eight significant collocation measures included four positive coefficient
collocation predictors. These were the rounded-up logit coefficients for:

- Mean MI for noun subject–verb combinations ('Mean MI nsubj') ($\beta = 0.330$,
  SE = 0.013, $z = 2.616$, $p = 0.008$);

Table 16 Converted odds ratios for mixed effects model with final grade

Predictor	Logit Coefficients	Std. Error	z-value	Pr(>|z|)	Odds Ratio	95% CIs	
						2.5%	97.5%
Mean LLR^2 amod	−0.206	0.067	−3.101	0.019	0.861	0.714	0.927
Mean MI nsubj	0.327	0.125	2.616	0.009	1.387	1.086	1.773
Mean Delta P w2|w1 nsubj	−0.202	0.090	−2.254	0.024	0.817	0.686	0.974
Mean t-score nsubj	−0.252	0.104	−2.433	0.015	0.777	0.634	0.952
Mean MI dobj	0.202	0.074	2.718	0.006	1.223	1.058	1.415
Mean Delta P w1|w2 dobj	−0.149	0.070	−2.118	0.034	0.862	0.751	0.989
Amod RTTR	0.196	0.077	2.552	0.011	1.216	1.046	1.414
Nsubj RTTR	0.135	0.075	1.795	0.072	1.144	0.988	1.325
Language_status2	0.376	0.155	2.426	0.015	1.457	1.075	1.974

Table 17 Converted thresholds and logit coefficients for mixed effects model with final grade

Threshold Coefficient		Logit Coefficients	Odds Ratio	95% CI	
				2.5%	97.5%
7|8	C– | C	–3.402	0.033	0.022	0.050
8|9	C | C+	–2.707	0.067	0.048	0.093
9|10	B– | B+	–2.039	0.130	0.099	0.171
10|11	B+| B–	–1.321	0.267	0.215	0.331
11|12	B– | B+	–0.563	0.569	0.478	0.678
12|13	B+| A–	0.135	1.144	0.971	1.348
13|14	A– | A	1.165	3.206	2.610	3.939
14|15	A | A+	2.181	8.859	6.674	11.759

- Mean MI for verb–direct object noun combinations ('Mean MI dobj') ($\beta = 0.201$, SE $= 0.074$, $z = 2.718$, $p = 0.007$);
- Adjective–noun diversity ('Amod RTTR') ($\beta = 0.196$, SE $= 0.007$, $z = 2.552$, $p = 0.002$);
- Noun–subject diversity ('Nsubj RTTR') ($\beta = 0.135$, SE $= 0.075$, $z = 1.795$, $p = 0.007$).

As the only non-linguistic predictor, language status ('Language_status2') was also significant ($\beta = 0.376$, SE $= 0.155$, $z = 2.426$, $p = 0.015$).

The remaining four negative coefficient predictors were the logit coefficients for:

- Mean LLR^2 adjective–noun combinations ('Mean LLR^2 amod') ($\beta = -0.206$, SE $= 0.067$, $z = -3.101$, $p = 0.002$);
- Mean Delta P for word 2\| word 1 noun–subject verb combinations ('Mean Delta P w2 \| w1 nsubj') ($\beta = -0.201$, SE $= 0.009$, $z = -2.254$, $p = 0.024$);
- Mean t-score noun–subject verb combinations ('Mean t-score nsubj') ($\beta = -0.252$, SE $= -0.103$, $z = -2.433$, $p = 0.015$);
- Mean Delta P w1\|w2 verb–direct object–noun combinations ('Mean Delta P w1\| w2 dobj') ($\beta = -0.149$, SE $= 0.007$, $z = -2.118$, $p = 0.034$).

Following advice in statistics literature (e.g., Liu, 2016; Winter, 2020), the logit odds were converted into odds ratios to aid interpretation. The key to interpreting these odds lies in whether the odds ratio is more than or less than 1. When less than 1, the odds of being beyond or at a particular grade level are expressed as being lower. When more than 1, the odds of being beyond or at a particular grade level are expressed as being higher. The model output in Figure 4 is therefore interpreted as follows.

For the positive coefficients, the odds of being at or beyond a particular final grade score were 1.387 times higher with a one unit increase in the mean MI noun–subject–verb combinations ('Mean MI nsubj'); 1.223 times higher with a one-unit increase in the mean MI for verb–direct object noun combinations ('Mean MI dobj'); 1.216 times higher with a one-unit increase in the adjective–noun diversity ('Amod RTTR'); 1.144 times higher with a one-unit increase in the noun–verb diversity ('Nsubj RTTR'). In other words, the use of higher 'Mean MI nsubj', 'Mean MI dobj', 'Amod RTTR', and 'Nsubj RTTR' means there are higher odds of texts being awarded a higher final grade score.

Those collocation predictors with negative logit coefficients can be interpreted as follows. In terms of the odds ratio (OR), the odds of being at or beyond a particular 'Final_Grade' score are lower by a factor of 0.861 for a one-unit increase in the mean Loglikelhood Ratio Squared adjective–noun combinations ('mean LLR^2 amod'). The odds of being beyond a particular final grade score are lower by a factor of 0.817 for a one-unit increase in the mean Delta P w2| w1 for noun–direct object–verb combinations ('Mean Delta P w2|w1 nsubj'). The odds of being beyond a particular final grade score are lower by a factor of 0.777 for a one-unit increase in the mean t-score noun–subject–verb combinations ('Mean t-score nsubj'). The odds of being beyond a particular final grade score are lower by a factor of 0.862 for a one-unit increase in the mean Delta P w1|w2 noun–direct object–verb combinations ('Mean Delta P w1|w2 dobj'). These results indicate that the odds of being at or beyond a particular grade level are lower with a one-unit increase in the predictors of 'Mean LLR^2 amod', 'Mean Delta P w2|w1 nsubj', 'Mean t-score Nsubj', and 'Mean Delta P w1|w2 dobj'.

In the mixed effects model, 'Language_status2' indicates that the odds of non-native writers being beyond a particular grade level were 1.457 times greater than native writers. It is important to recognise the importance of this contextual finding and place it side by side with the findings of those that were positive linguistic coefficients. These results seem to indicate that in the case of the positive coefficients, there is a similar size of odds for grade increase with language status and both amod and nsubj diversity with the odds higher for language status, helping put into perspective two things. First, that there is a tendency for the odds of a grade increase to be shaped by multiple linguistic and non-linguistic variables, and second, in this case the non-linguistic predictor has slightly higher odds of grade increase than the linguistic predictors.

6.3 Model Validity

In terms of how confident we can be that these results reflect the 'true' odds of 'Final_Grade' increasing or decreasing, an examination of the 95 per cent confidence intervals (CI) in Table 15 indicates that all odds ratios for the measures fall within the CI range. This means that if the model was repeatedly estimated, the true odds would lie in the same range, 95 per cent of the time, thus giving confidence in the model.

We can also examine the threshold coefficients that make up the cumulative model. In Table 16, it is important to illuminate the different logit and odds ratios that appear across these comparisons. In Table 17, we see that the logit odds are negative for grade comparisons 7–13, the odds of the predictors, increasing grades decrease. There is a noticeable shift in direction at the two highest grade levels, that of comparisons between 13 and 14, and 14 and 15, whereby the logit odds and the odds ratio become positive. This appears to suggest that predictors have increased odds of increasing grade particularly at these higher levels.

Overall, the mixed effects model shows that the predictors of 'Mean MI nsubj', 'Mean MI dobj', and the amod (Amod RTTR) and nsubj (Nsubj RTTR) diversity dependencies have higher odds of increasing final grade scores.

In contrast, the predictors of the 'Mean LLR^2 amod', 'Mean Delta P w2|w1 Nsubj', 'Mean t-score Nsubj', and 'Mean Delta P w1|w2 Dobj' have lower odds of increasing final grade scores. To some extent this mirrors the findings from Paquot (2019) who also found support for the MI as did other studies (e.g., Bestgen & Granger, 2014; Durrant & Schmitt, 2009; Granger & Bestgen, 2014). However, in the case of this FYC context, support for the MI is for nsubj and dobj dependencies rather than amod dependencies. It appears that in the FYC context, rather than being more likely to award higher grades for more sophisticated amod dependencies like Paquot (2019), the odds of FYC raters awarding higher grades to more diverse amod and nsubj use is greater. It is also worth bearing in mind that since these diversity measures contain both dependencies that would reach or not reach collocation status according to past MI thresholds, then it seems it is more likely that raters tend to be overall influenced by the variation of dependency types and to a lesser extent their average sophistication.

To evaluate the goodness-of-fit for the mixed effects models, there are several statistics available (e.g., see Levshina, 2015; Liu, 2016). Although traditional modelling literature has often cited the R^2 value to give an estimate of how much variance in grade is explained by a particular model, such an estimate is not recommended for this kind of logistic regression.

Levshina (2015) comments on the use of Pseudo R^2 as a measure of goodness-of-fit. Like many others (e.g., Field et al., 2012; Liu, 2016), she notes that in logistic regression models, the value of the R^2 is often lower than the R^2 in linear regression, even if the quality of models is comparable. Equally, Levshina (2015) notes that the Pseudo R^2 is less conceptually clear than the R^2 from linear regression. It is often misinterpreted as being the same concept as the linear R^2;

however, this is disputed by Hosmer and Lemeshow (2000), who have made direct criticisms of the statistic. For these reasons, the ordinal package used in this study does not support the use of the Pseudo R^2.[1]

Considering this, the models created in this Element are simply evaluated by looking at the AIC values. The inclusion of the individual writer as a random variable results in a model which is more able to explain variation in grade, as indicated by its lower AIC value: 3598.11 compared with the fixed model only, which has an AIC value of 3599.58. This gives us confidence that the modelling type is a more appropriate way to model score variation than previously used linear regression techniques. Similar results have also been reported in Haberman and Sinharay (2010).

6.4 Conclusions

This section highlights the value of mixed effects modelling as a method of exploring relationships between collocation and writing quality, as well as a number of writing context and learner-specific variables. It highlights the contrasting relationships that exist between the individual association measures and writing quality grades, as well as the relationships that exist between measures of diversity and writing quality. It also furthers our understanding of how the language background of the writer has a relationship with writing quality grades.

Section 7 explores these results in more detail and seeks to uncover possible explanations for these statistical results by looking at the rhetorical functions that these word combinations perform.

MODELLING HIGHLIGHTS

- Random variation in the form of individual writers accounted for most of the variation in scores.
- Higher odds of grade increase were associated with higher mean MI for noun–subject verb and verb–direct object noun combination; higher diversity for adjective–noun and noun–direct object combinations.
- Lower odds of grade increase were associated with higher mean LLR² ratio for adjective–noun combinations, Delta P w2|w1 noun–direct verb combinations, Delta P w1|w2 verb–direct object combinations, and t-score noun–direct object–verb combinations.
- Higher odds of grade increase were associated with writers who were second language writers.

---

[1] Rune Haubo Bojesen Christensen, personal communication, 2020.

7 Study Three: Qualitative Understandings
of Writing Quality
7.1 Overview of Section

While study two presented a quantitative measurement of variables that may shape writing quality scores, the final study of this Element also engages with the second question through a qualitative lens. In looking qualitatively at the FYC essays, the analysis uncovers possible reasons for the statistical patterns uncovered in study two.

This section carries out a qualitative analysis of high- and low-scoring association measures and high- and low-scoring diversity across the FYC corpus. We focus on answering the following questions that arose from the role of association measures in the statistical modelling:

- Why might higher mean MI noun subject–verb (nsubj) combinations have higher odds of increasing grades?
- Why might higher mean MI direct object–verb (dobj) combinations have higher odds of increasing grades?
- Why might higher mean LLR^2 adjective–noun (amod) combinations have lower odds of increasing grades?
- Why might higher mean Delta P w2|w1 noun subject–verb (nsubj) combinations have lower odds of increasing grades?
- Why might higher mean Delta P w1|w2 direct object–verb (dobj) combinations have lower odds of increasing grades?
- Why might higher mean t-score noun subject–verb (nsubj) combinations have lower odds of increasing grades?

The section also addresses the following question that arose from the role of diversity measures in the statistical modelling:

- Why might higher amod RTTR and nsubj RTTR diversity have higher odds of increasing grades?

To help answer these questions, Tables 18–29 highlight high- and low-scoring combinations on each measure. Each table shows the top or bottom five ranked examples on a particular measure from the FYC corpus. In each case, only collocations occurring in more than three independent texts were included. This allowed us to explore how high- and low-scoring frequent combinations (i.e., those occurring in multiple texts) may be used and how this use may be an indicator of language use that FYC raters appear to value or devalue. A fuller set of dependencies is included as supplementary materials on https://leemccallum/net/resources.

Table 18 High-scoring MI nsubj dependencies

Nsubj Dependency	MI Score
paper__nn_:_focus__vb	4.41
paper__nn_:_discuss__vb	4.30
evidence__nn_:_support__vb	4.28
paper__nn_:_address__vb	4.25
Lesson__nn_:_provide__vb	3.49

Table 19 Low-scoring MI nsubj dependencies

Nsubj Dependency	MI Score
goal__nn_:_be__vb	−1.89
possibility__nn_:_be__vb	−1.75
explanation__nn_:_be__vb	−1.34
study__nn_:_provide__vb	0.66
use__nn_:_make__vb	1.02

7.2 Positive Relationships between Association Measures and Writing Quality

This section examines the use of high- and low-scoring MI combinations to offer explanation as to why high-scoring mean MI values may have greater odds of increasing grades.

7.2.1 Why Might Higher Mean MI Nsubj Combinations Have Higher Odds of Increasing Grades?

Tables 18 and 19 offer an important understanding of high- and low-scoring MI units. Table 18 highlights how high-scoring combinations comprise combinations which have clearly identifiable rhetorical functions. Combinations such as 'paper__nn_:_focus__vb' and other 'paper + verb' combinations are used to set out what the essay intends to do. These functions are shown in examples [6]–[9], taken from different FYC essays.

[6]   This **paper** will **focus** on the two most popular opinions, for and against players linked to steroids being treated the dame for consideration for the Hall of Fame; then find common ground between the two sides so that there may be a compromise.

[7]   This **paper** will **focus** on different views on air pollution between China National Chemical Corporation in Beijing and local citizens.

[8]   This **paper** will specifically **focus** on efforts for animal rights in the entertain-
        ment industry, that being animals in zoos.

[9]   To sum up, this **paper** would **discuss** how social media affect higher education.

The low-scoring MI combinations shown in Table 19 highlight how these
combinations comprise pairings of frequent lexical verbs such as 'be' and 'have',
which can have many other word partners. In the FYC corpus, they do not appear
to perform clear rhetorical functions or give an indication of genre or discipline,
when compared with high-scoring combinations, as examples [10]–[12] indicate.

[10]   The parties should not call for complete abolishment of standardized tests in the
        college application system: the main **goal** of the reform should **be** to shift the
        focus of college applications from standardized tests to a more well-rounded
        form of student evaluation.

[11]   Uber's main **goal** would **be** to achieve better public relations due to the political
        firestorm caused by taxi companies suing Uber for the variety of reasons above.

[12]   The **possibility** in order to help treat the veterans for post-traumatic stress
        disorder would **be** to have them go through a mental evaluation.

These findings align with Paquot (2018, 2019), who also commented that
combinations which receive higher MI scores tend to have greater identifiable
disciplinary/genre functions, while those with lower scores tend to comprise
word pairs which are less exclusive and less tied to particular disciplines or
genres. This observation may indicate that FYC raters value rhetorical functions
being performed using exclusive pairings.

7.2.2 Why Might Higher Mean MI Dobj Combinations Have Higher Odds of Increasing Text Grades?

Tables 20 and 21 show high- and low-scoring dobj dependencies. Table 20
shows a range of high-scoring MI dobj dependencies. Many of these also
perform textual functions and/or are used to directly meet the task aims (e.g.,
in example 13, 'bridge__vb_:_gap__nn' is used to show how the two sides can
reach a compromise, the requirement of the ENC 1102 task, while examples
[14]–[17] focus on illuminating a particular issue/benefits of a particular
approach, or presenting different stakeholder initiatives).

[13]   If not through social change then through legal changes, such as the bill in
        Maryland, can **bridge** the **gap** between the two sides on this issue.

[14]   The National Education Association withholds an ongoing commitment to
        bridge the **gap** between implementation and standards, through curriculum,
        training and support.

Table 20 High-scoring MI dobj dependencies

Dobj Dependencies	MI Score
bridge__vb_:_gap__nn	11.23
shed__vb_:_light__nn	11.05
take__vb_:_course__nn	10.75
steal__vb_:_money__nn	9.79
prevent__vb_:_fraud__nn	9.40

Table 21 Low-scoring MI dobj dependencies

Dobj Dependencies	MI Score
have__vb_:_value__nn	−1.19
have__vb_:_role__nn	−1.00
have__vb_:_experience__nn	−0.78
have__vb_:_ability__nn	−0.74
have__vb_:_time__nn	−0.60

[15]   Not only this, it will also **shed light** on work-life balance, lack of funds and survival in recessions and how it is confronted by corporate owners to be successful in the competitive market.

[16]   The main goal of this mission will be to **shed light** on the icy potential habitability, but it could also search for signs of alien life.

[17]   They also work to improve the legal system to prevent these false convictions and to **shed light** on the inhumanity of the death penalty.

Many of the low-scoring MI dobj dependencies in Table 21 were found to perform a variety of rhetorical functions, as examples [18]–[21] show, including bringing the reader into the text by posing a question (e.g., [18]) setting out the implications of a compromise (e.g., examples [19]–[21]); however, the dependencies comprise highly frequent lexical verbs (e.g., have), which can have many other alternative partnering nouns, meaning the dependencies here are less exclusive.

[18]   Do all people have rights to **have** this **value**?

[19]   This allows the reader to feel a sense of community regarding individuals across the globe, along with a sense of community between people and nature, all of which Monsanto is claiming to **have** a **role** in making happen.

[20]   If they both choose to work together in the near future, the life of student athletes would be the best it has ever been and athletes would **have** a more meaningful college **experience**.

[21]   This will allow them to **have** more **time** to focus on the classes they are taking to ensure they get a good grade, more free time, less stress, and it will allow them to be involved in more organizations and possibly take leadership roles or internships to prepare for their future.

This contrast again aligns with Paquot (2018, 2019), who comments that many low-scoring combinations comprise 'nuclear' or basic units of vocabulary and their use does not indicate affiliation with a particular genre or academic writing more broadly. The observations across high- and low-scoring combinations in the FYC corpus also raise the possibility that raters may value writers performing rhetorical functions through the use of word combinations which are more exclusive. The next sub-sections turn to consider the reasons why some association measures have less chance of increasing grade scores.

7.3 Negative Relationships between Association Measures and Writing Quality

This section examines the use of association measures which have lower odds of increasing grade scores.

7.3.1 Why Might Higher Mean Loglikelihood Ratio Squared Amod Combinations Have Lower Odds of Increasing Text Grades?

Looking at dependencies which had less chance of increasing grade, the list of LLR^2 amod combinations in Table 22 shows high-scoring combinations, and Table 23 shows the low-scoring combinations. Table 22's combinations have a clear connection to the topics of the essays; while Table 23's combinations are less specific and comprise more generic words such as 'many', 'good', 'other', and 'different'.

Since loglikelihood ratio measures operate as significance measures, higher scoring combinations represent stronger evidence that the pairing is significant. It is also worth noting that high-scoring combinations here are obviously closely related to the topics themselves. It could be that higher scoring combinations are devalued by raters because they represent basic collocation choices. It is worth bearing in mind that variations of measures of loglikelihood ratios have been found to perform well in collocation identification tasks which compare association measures to 'gold standard' human identification and/or sources of collocation/word inventories (e.g., see Evert, 2009). Evert (2009) also notes that loglikelihood ratio measures appear to flag up 'typical' or 'plausible' collocations.

Table 22 High-scoring LLR^2 amod dependencies

Amod Dependency	LLR^2 Score
High__jj_:_school__nn	1,930.80
Domestic__jj_:_violence__nn	1,331.51
Renewable__jj_:_energy__nn	1,325.69
Social__jj_:_movement__nn	1,155.75
Great__jj_:_deal__nn	870.40

Table 23 Low-scoring LLR^2 amod dependencies

Amod Dependency	LLR^2 Score
Other__jj_:_health__nn	7.87
Good__jj_:_student__nn	7.58
Many__jj_:_group__nn	7.56
Different__jj_:_system__nn	7.33
Other__jj_:_process__nn	7.03

With this in mind, it is possible then for FYC raters that these obvious or typical combinations are devalued as too simple choices for the tasks being completed.

7.3.2 Why Might Higher Mean Delta P Combinations Have Lower Odds of Increasing Text Grades?

Similarly, the same can be said for Delta P measures. Little previous research helps guide an evaluation of these combinations since in the first and second language literature, and the wider computational linguistics literature, use of this association measure is only just starting to emerge. However, when ranked from highest to lowest, interesting contrasts emerge. High scoring Delta P combinations are shown in Table 24 for Delta P w2 | w1 nsubj dependencies, while low-scoring Delta P w2 | w1 nsubj dependencies are shown in Table 25.

Tables 26 and 27 show that a similar picture emerges for Delta P w1| w2 dobj dependencies. The high-scoring combinations in Table 26 show some cross-over with high-scoring MI combinations. For example, combinations such as 'shed__vb_:_light__nn' feature highly on both lists as does 'bridge__vb_:_gap__nn'; however, there are a number of combinations which have highly ranking Delta P score but much lower MI scores. For example, comparing both the ranking of the MI and Delta P scores, entries such as 'solve__vb_:_problem__nn' and 'play__vb_:_role__nn' feature in the top ten highly ranked combinations for

Table 24 High-scoring Delta P w2 | w1 nsubj
dependencies

Nsubj Dependency	Delta P Score
resistance__nn_:_be__vb	0.81
measure__nn_:_have__vb	0.76
belief__nn_:_be__vb	0.73
program__nn_:_have__vb	0.70
fear__nn_:_be__vb	0.63

Table 25 Low- scoring Delta P w2 | w1 nsubj
dependencies

Nsubj Dependency	Delta P Score
student__nn_:_come__vb	−0.001
thinking__nn_:_be__vb	−0.001
student__nn_:_provide__vb	−0.001
graduate__nn_:_have__vb	−0.001
wave__nn_:_be__vb	−0.001

Table 26 High-scoring Delta P w1|w2 dobj
dependencies

Dobj Dependency	Delta P Score
shed__vb_:_light__nn	0.29
bridge__vb_:_gap__nn	0.21
reduce__vb_:_cost__nn	0.22
have__vb_:_sense__nn	0.22
create__vb_:_space__nn	0.21

Delta P, but when examining the MI scores, these same combinations only feature among the top forty entries. This raises questions about the relationship between the property of exclusivity that is being measured by the MI measure, and the weight being placed on word 1 of the combination in the Delta P w1 w2 dobj dependencies. These differences in ranking are worth further examination, possibly with consideration for what cognitively may be being represented for word combinations where word 1 in the combination is more likely to attract word 2. It is also worth

Table 27 Low-scoring Delta P w1|w2 dobj
dependencies

Dobj Dependency	Delta P Score
be__vb_:__ word__nn	−0.033
be__vb_:__ class__nn	−0.034
be__vb_:__ number__nn	−0.034
be__vb_:__ student__nn	−0.034
be__vb_:__ example__nn	−0.034

considering how and why word 1 being more likely to attract word 2 has a lesser chance of grade increases. The answers to these queries may lie in considering the type-token distribution which has been captured by the lexical gravity measure (Brezina et al., 2015). This measure can capture the strength of a collocational relationship but also establish the level of competition for the slot around the node word from other collocate types. This kind of insight may offer us a route into intersections between the property of exclusivity that is measured by the MI and the property of directionality that is captured by the Delta P. Understanding the competition between words to 'fill' the slot would also allow us to make better inferences about the types of language choices students are making, the influence these choices have on raters, and how much these choices appear to be valued by raters.

A connected possible explanation for the Delta P results here may lie in the notion of what constitutes a 'good' cue. As Schneider (2020) comments, Delta P is a measure of cue validity because it measures how strongly two events are linked. It works on evaluating how reliably a specific event (event 1) triggers another event (event 2), considering how likely event 2 is to occur after any other event. In this sense, Ellis and Ferreira-Junior (2009) have discussed the idea of 'good' cues and the impact they have on word combinations and predictability. They note that a good cue is 'one where, whenever, it is present the outcome pertains, and whenever absent, the outcome does not' (Ellis & Ferreira-Junior, 2009, p. 197). In language learning, they promote Delta P as a good measure of cue learnability where higher Delta P scores indicate a greater likelihood of the outcome, given the presence of the cue. Relating this notion back to our findings that Delta P measures have less odds of increasing grades, it may be that learners are using cues which attract obvious noun/verb choices, and this obvious language use is being devalued by FYC raters. In this respect, one aspect of future research to move forward our understandings of these relationships would be to look at how verb and noun 'cues' are being used by learners, and how they are judged by raters would be beneficial in future work.

7.3.3 Why Might Higher Mean T-Score Nsubj Combinations Have Lower Odds of Increasing Grades?

An examination of the negative coefficient t-score nsubj dependency measure in Tables 28 and 29 also illuminates a similar picture to other negative predictors. Both high-and low-scoring combinations show combinations that comprise two highly frequent words (i.e., nouns such as 'people' and verbs such as 'have' and 'be'). This negative result and inspection of high-and low-scoring combinations makes intuitive sense since these combinations are not particularly indicative of academic writing or genres and are not found across multiple modes of communication and contexts.

7.4 Positive Relationships between Diversity and Writing Quality Grades

7.4.1 Why Might Higher Amod RTTR and Nsubj RTTR Diversity Have Higher Odds of Increasing Grades?

A third set of important findings from the statistical modelling was the role played by amod and nsubj diversity measures. Both measures were found to increase the odds of higher grades in the FYC context. In attempting to understand why this diversity leads to higher odds of a grade increase, a qualitative inspection of

Table 28 High-scoring T-score nsubj dependencies

Nsubj Dependency	T-score Score
analysis__nn_:_be__vb	12.22
participant__nn_:_be__vb	11.46
theory__nn_:_be__vb	11.13
study__nn_:_have__vb	11.08
model__nn_:_be__vb	10.96

Table 29 Low-scoring T-score nsubj dependencies

Nsubj Dependency	T-score Score
energy__nn_:_have__vb	−16.53
organisation__nn_:_have__vb	−16.59
school__nn_:_be__vb	−17.05
time__nn_:_have__vb	−17.07
government__nn_:_be__vb	−18.72

texts with high- and low-amod and nsubj diversity was carried out. It should be noted that in many cases, higher amod and nsubj diversity were found irrespective of text length in higher graded texts. Example texts A and B in Figures 5 and 6 respectively, show this trend and the different uses of amod dependencies. Text A shows how a high-scoring diversity text uses many dependencies to perform different rhetorical functions and creates arguments; Text B, a lower scoring text, shows how the use of fewer dependencies is related to a narrower range of rhetorical functions and arguments. It is also worth highlighting here that these two examples at opposite ends of the diversity scale are equal in word count and therefore the issue of text length and diversity is accounted for in this case.

It should also be highlighted that Text A contained many instances of amod dependencies which could have been considered specific topic/discipline items

---

Text A: High amod RTTR (dependencies as retrieved by the Stanford Parser)

In the 1960s people became interested in study of whales and dolphins in the wild and spent **significant time** observing their behavior. Over the **next** twenty **years**, they grew to know cetaceans a little, but that little was enough for the beginning of speculation on the role of culture in their lives (Whitehead 2015). In **early 2000s**, it was stated that **marine mammals** could be claimed as species with **cultural lives** (Norris 2002). It means that whales and dolphins can have **progressive cognitive abilities, developed personalities**, and **broad abilities** of communications and cooperations. Modern studies provide **credible evidences** to support this theory. However, some aspects of the research such as the reasons for a **huge size** of **cetacean brain body** and the lack of **neural base** are too challenging to be considered as absolutely reliable. Additionally, some scientists present **alternative point** of view on the subject.

(Root TTR: 7.01; Grade A+, L2 writer, text length: 1,377 words).

Figure 5 Text A high amod RTTR

Text B: Low amod RTTR (dependencies as retrieved by the Stanford Parser)

The history of **African Americans** and their experience with the **American justice system** has been a long one. During the mid-too **late twentieth century**, America experienced a **great deal** of racism. **African Americans** were viewed as worthless and experienced a **great deal** of racism. This country underwent a lot of events due to this situation. However, as time went on, African Americans were soon granted more freedom and more rights. This is evident in the fact that had an **African American** hold **office** as the President of the United States for 8 years, some of our well- known **political figures** within America are black, and some of our **well-known entertainers** are black. Because this country is ultimately dividing and repressing into its **old ways**, America should unify in order to minimize and hopefully stop instances of **racial injustice** between government and minorities.

(Root TTR: 4.70; Grade C-, L1 writer, text length: 1, 377 words).

Figure 6 Text B low amod RTTR

(e.g., neural base). It is also worth commenting on the impression writer of Text A creates on the reader as they appear to have clear control of using these dependencies both for creating arguments and for particular rhetorical functions. Use of the dependencies is both varied and accurate to give a sense of clear ownership of the text and attempting to meet the task requirements by setting up the issue as debatable/controversial. In Text B, many of the amod dependencies used are repeated across adjacent sentences (e.g., great deal) and are simply descriptive. Equally, the overall tone of the text is subjective and bordering on emotive rather than building on a particular stance through academic argument. This lack of diversity and effective use may be factors that raters devalue in their judgements. It is also worth commenting that the use of amod dependencies is embedded around reference to academic literature in Text A, while in Text B, where amod dependencies are used and used with variation, they do not appear to be used in relation to use of source materials to support their claims. Overall, these issues of variation, rhetorical function, and intended meaning/tone are worth considering as factors which raters judge negatively.

For nsubj diversity, a similar pattern was present, as shown in Figures 7 and 8 for with Texts C and D. Text C shows the use of varied nsubj dependencies to promote the benefits of a vegetarian diet, while in Text D the dependencies used are not directly linked to the writer performing a particular rhetorical function or achieving a particular rhetorical effect with the issue of euthanasia. Like the contrast between Text A and B, nsubj appears being used in the higher scoring text to construct a literature-led argument. For example, note the use

---

Text C: High nsubj RTTR (dependencies as retrieved by the Stanford Parser)

More specifically, the vegetarian **diet** can **help** those who may be at greater risk for developing common heart diseases or diabetes. For people who struggle with these health issues, but do not wish to go on medication, it is beneficial for them to start a vegetarian diet. For those wishing to embark on the vegetarian diet though, it is important to consult a doctor or registered dietician before making the change. Certain health issues can develop if precautions are not made during the diet, especially during high metabolic periods of life. Recent **studies** have **shown** that some health **issues** may **occur** during specific stages of life where high metabolic **activity occurs**. One study in particular done by Dr. T. Nguyen, who has a doctorate in medicine, showed that the vegetarian **diet** may **affect** bone mass. In the paper, the **author stated** that ratio of animal protein to vegetable protein had a significant effect on bone loss at the femoral (Nguyen). When Dr. **Nguyen mentions** the femoral neck, he is talking about the hip joint. **Weakness** in the hip joint can **cause** a lot of discomfort and is common in older patients.

(Root TTR: 3.16, Grade A-, L1 writer, text length: 1,387 words)

Figure 7 Text C high nsubj RTTR

Text D: Low nsubj RTTR (dependencies as retrieved by the Stanford Parser)

Euthanasia, or assisted suicide, has **caught** the attention of many scholars and physicians worldwide. Due to the controversy surrounding the topic on whether or not it is a basic right for a **person** to **have** the right to choose to be euthanized, the responses have been a mixture of both negative and positive feedback as **people sit** back and assess what it really means to euthanize a patient with a terminal illness. Euthanasia is not a morally problematic concept, but instead it should be seen as something that gives people relief. It relinquishes the burden that they have been carrying for so long, and allows them to finally receive the peace that they have sought out for. In regards to the controversy surrounding euthanasia, or assisted suicide, it is a fundamental right that should be for everyone, therefore it should not be seen as an ethical or morally damaging issue. In an article entitled, and Assisted Suicide from a Confucian Moral it focuses on the three concepts that argue euthanasia to be morally right. of the concepts is mercy, the other is preventing indignity, and the last one is the argument of (Ping- Cheung Lo 60).

(Root TTR: 1.13, Grade C+, L1 writer, text length: 1,343 words)

Figure 8 Text D low nsubj RTTR

of nsubj dependencies to discuss the work of Dr Ngyuen, while in the lower scoring text, the discussion is not as critical and is instead more descriptive of the study being used rather than fully successfully using the study to support their arguments.

Several other rhetorical functions were facilitated through the use of different amod and nsubj dependencies in high-scoring amod and nsubj diversity texts. A summary of these functions with dependencies retrieved by the parser is shown in examples [22]–[30].

- Setting out the issues with a topic over time:

[22]   The **first** recorded **usage** of marijuana dates all the way back to 10,000-Year World History of Hemp and 1) and continues to this **very day**. In **recent history**, the United States has had several states legalize the plant on different levels (recreational use, medicinal use, etc.).

- Generally critiquing the topic under study:

[23]   The **next few paragraphs** will be **describing** what happened in Ukraine prior and during the invasion, the failures and importance of energy between the EU and Russia, and why this is more then just a coincidence as **many critics** might **lead** you to believe'.

- Making reference to source-based evidence:

[24]   Nonetheless, the studies that have been conducted show empirical, **credible evidence** to support the medicinal benefits of marijuana for a variety of different patients and conditions.

- Showing support for the efforts of a particular stakeholder:

[25]   Government space agencies have rapidly and, for the **most part**, reliably developed technology that improves everyday life.

- Interpreting the evidence presented to support a point:

[26]   Dr. Davis results show that no matter the regulation provided the **public** will **abuse** of medical marijuana just as they had already abused of the drug in the 1920s'; Lovinger clarifies that, LSB, Cannabinoid receptors generally inhibits neuronal excitability and neurotransmitter (Lovinger 1156). What Dr. Lovinger is saying is that when the human body undergoes a treatment or use of marijuana, the **drug** does not **allow** for the nervous system to continue working in the ways that it should').

- Indicating that there are different sometimes opposing views on the topic:

[27]   There is another class of individuals that ignores the factual analysis and presents a **different perspective**.

[28]   The researchers have done their research about this subject in afflication with the university of Bergen and the institute of global health and community medicine in Bergen, and come to the assumption that using surrogates in communities such as India, with lower economy and a **different** cultural **view** on the role of females and pregnancy, is something they would strondly advise against.

- Highlighting the benefits of taking action:

[29]   In most aspects of life, a **common goal** can lead to an unexpected partnership.

[30]   The process has the advantage of being in its infancy and the potential to become an even more **accurate procedure.**

7.5 Discussion

The functional uses explored in Section 7.4 go *some* way to helping students meet the fundamental primary learning objectives of their programme. In the ENC 1101 task, they are expected to synthesise multiple stakeholder perspectives in the form of a literature review. In the ENC 1102 task, they are expected to balance the competing views expressed in the ENC 1101 task by attempting to show how stakeholders can reach a compromise (see Section 2). The examples show how the dependency types go *some* way to perhaps facilitating greater task achievement as students navigate the task of setting out the key arguments between stakeholders and then looking at how these stakeholders can reach a viable compromise.

These dependencies and their inter-related functions also appear to contribute towards students showing *critical thinking* in that students '*evaluate evidence, recognize and evaluate underlying assumptions, identify and evaluate chains of reasoning, and compose appropriately qualified and developed claims and generalizations*' (CWPA, 2014). The Postsecondary Framework for Success (CWPA et al., 2011) also describes how writers are asked to 'write texts for various audiences and purposes that are informed by research (e.g., to support ideas or positions, to illustrate alternative perspectives, to provide additional contexts').

These results also strengthen the points made by Aull (2015), who acknowledges that language patterns are not isolated structures that appear randomly but are instead linked to the macro-level writing processes/demands of the assignment whereby these patterns facilitate achieving the macro processes.

7.6 Conclusion

This study has helped highlight the importance of implementing a type of mixed effects modelling which accounts for the random effects structure of the sampling corpus and at the same time preserves the ordinal levels of the outcome/dependent variable. The analysis highlighted how a number of linguistic and non-linguistic fixed effects appeared to have the potential to increase or decrease the odds of essays being awarded higher or lower grades. However, an inspection of the threshold coefficients suggests that these effects are not uniform or operating in the same directions for all grade levels.

In relating findings from the statistical modelling to the literature, there is some support from the Element's findings for the comments made by Durrant and Brenchley (2021). Their analysis of L1 children's writing encouraged us to be cautious and appreciate that phraseological sophistication or indeed the phraseological complexity, when we include the sub-construct of diversity, is not a uniform construct that develops or is evaluated uniformly across educational contexts. The final section of this study illuminates the contributions to knowledge that the modelling has made and discusses what needs to be considered as a priority for future research.

QUALITATIVE HIGHLIGHTS

- Writers appear to use high- and low-scoring association measures to perform a variety of rhetorical functions with a degree of difference in how clearly these functions are connected to academic writing at large.
- The use of high-scoring MI combinations and the contrasting use of high-scoring t-score and LLR^2 ratio combinations indicate that student

writers appear to use higher scoring MI combinations along a cline of language that is known to be associated with academic language.

- For Delta P measures, there is a possibility that 'good' cues are not used by students, and this has an impact on rater judgements.
- The positive relationships between association measures and diversity and grades lead to questions about how these proxy measures may interact/combine to have a relationship with writing quality.

8 Conclusions

8.1 Overview of Section

This Element focussed on answering one central question: which linguistic and non-linguistic variables may play a role in shaping the writing quality scores awarded to student essays in an FYC writing context?

In doing so, we also engaged with two subquestions which occupy space in the collocation–grade relationship literature: (i) how can we choose appropriate measures of collocation? and (ii) how can we measure and understand the potential role of different linguistic and non-linguistic variables in an appropriate way? The following sections summarise the key results obtained from our work, acknowledges its limitations, and discusses avenues for future research in FYC contexts.

8.2 Findings for Question 1: How Can We Choose Appropriate Measures of Collocation?

The cluster analysis found that measures in Cluster 1 tap into the property of exclusivity. Other clusters illuminated different properties, including highly frequent pairings, as illuminated by the t-score in Cluster 5 and aspects of directionality in Clusters 4 and 5. Overall, the cluster analysis was able to shed numerical and visual light onto the relationships between different association measures. In total, six measures were identified as distinct: the MI, the geometric mean, the LLR^2, the Delta P w2| w1, Delta P w1|w2, and the t-score. These six measures were used in study two to answer question 2.

8.3 Findings for Question 2: How Can We Measure and Understand the Potential Role of Different Linguistic and Non-linguistic Variables in an Appropriate Way?

A regression model known as a cumulative links or probability odds model was used to answer question 2. We chose this model because it could recognise grade scores as ordinal variables as well as incorporate interval and categorical predictor variables. This model has not featured much in learner writing research, and in drawing attention to such a model, we hope the learner writing community explores possible future avenues for working with this model.

The model highlighted that the Mean MI for nsubj dependencies and the Mean MI for dobj dependencies had higher odds of increasing grades.

The model also highlighted that the following linguistic predictors had lower odds of increasing grades:

- The mean LLR^2 for amod dependencies
- The mean Delta P for word 2 | word 1 nsubj dependencies
- The mean Delta P for word 1 | word 2 dobj dependencies
- The mean t-score for nsubj dependencies.

Overall, the model contributed to understanding the relationship between collocations and writing quality in different ways. It reiterated the important role that the MI, LLR^2, t-score, and Delta P may have in evaluating learner language. Although these association measures varied in their significance and direction, they all had higher or lower odds of a grade increase with their use.

The model also highlighted that the status of the writer as a second language writer had higher odds of increasing writing quality scores. When examining the odds ratios of the linguistic and non-linguistic predictors, it is important to interpret the linguistic predictors as having at least a similar effect on grade level as the non-linguistic predictor of language status. In fact, the odds ratio of language status was higher than the linguistic predictors. This finding offers an important glimpse into underlying FYC grading practices.

Several reasons may account for the language status of the writer being significant. Although it could be argued that the reason for this result is that raters could sub-consciously favour non-native writers, it is also possible that they are more likely to receive higher grades because they have had more exposure to writing through pre-university preparation courses and are therefore more in tune with writing for an audience and writing conventions (Lee, 2019). It is also possible that non-native writers have higher odds of receiving a higher grade because of the make-up of the raters. It is a feature of the FYC environment that essays are graded by instructors with mixed experience levels. At USF there are GTAs with far less experience than other faculty members, and while it may be attested that rater experience is a factor in rater judgements, the result in this FYC context contrasts with much of the previous literature which has found that inexperienced raters are actually more severe in their rating until they receive training to balance out their subjective views (e.g., Weigle, 1999). Equally, while previous research has found that non-native writing has been consistently graded lower than native writing (Huang & Foote, 2010), the FYC result obtained here seems to indicate that rating behaviour is context sensitive.

The final study in the Element also added to understandings of the relationships between linguistic predictors and writing quality scores by carrying out a qualitative analysis on high- and low-association measure scoring dependencies. This analysis found connections between how high- and low-association measure scoring dependencies were used to perform key FYC rhetorical goals. This included how high-scoring MI nsubj and dobj dependencies were used to introduce the focus of essays and emphasise the goal of compromising between stakeholders. For association measures with lower odds of a grade increase, dependencies comprised of more frequent generic words which were perhaps perceived by raters as being obvious ways of creating meaning.

High scoring amod and nsubj diversity texts also showed evidence of dependencies being used to perform particular rhetorical functions, including setting out issues with the topic over time and critiquing the topic, referring to sources as evidence, showing support for a particular stakeholder, capturing the range of different positions/views held about the topic, and emphasising the benefits of taking action/moving towards a compromise between stakeholders.

The study also adds weight to previous phraseology grade work in that it also finds that relationships between collocation and writing quality are not homogeneous but instead context specific, with other grading factors also playing a role in final grade allocation alongside the use of collocations (e.g., in line with Durrant & Brenchley, 2021).

Although the present study aligns with previous work in supporting the MI and t-score measures, the respective dependencies that have been illuminated are different. This Element also supports the diversity of amod and nsubj dependencies as having greater odds of increasing grade scores. However, there are several differences in the Element's methods and context that need to be acknowledged as potentially contributing to these differences. One such difference is that the Element is based on dependency types as opposed to the use of adjacent pairs which have been automatically extracted in much of the previous literature (except for recent studies such as Jiang et al., 2021 and Paquot, 2018, 2019, who also focus on dependencies).

Another reason for different results lies in the types of texts analysed. In previous studies, there has been a focus on second language proficiency where evaluations are concerned with whether or not students' proficiency is adequate enough for university study. This was the case in both Garner et al.'s (2019, 2020) studies of the Korean placement test. The texts in this Element are extended essays which have been drafted and reviewed by instructors and peers. This type of writing differs from much of the literature which has involved short, timed writing (e.g., Garner et al.'s (2019, 2020) placement tests were timed as were the descriptive essays in Bestgen and Granger (2014). Finally, Paquot's (2018, 2019) work also differs from the present context by focussing on coursework texts written by postgraduate linguistics students who were evaluated under the CEFR scale.

The FYC context also evaluates a broad range of rhetorical and curriculum goals as opposed to the narrow focus on ESL courses that have been studied before. These types of different foci have been highlighted by Lee (2019), who notes that ESL courses cover how to write and place emphasis on explicit language use, while FYC courses orient towards assessing multiple rhetorical goals and favour implicit language use.

8.4 Implications for the FYC Programme at USF

Overall, the methods and studies in this Element have contributed to a wider drive in the FYC literature to complement composition instruction with that of language support. The Element promotes the use of advanced statistical techniques to understand how aspects of collocation may contribute to grade allocation and ultimately facilitate students' task completion and achievement of FYC programme goals. This Element supports the work of other scholars who have stated that language support should be embedded into FYC student learning, and more broadly FYC programme outcomes and frameworks (e.g., Aull, 2015, 2017, 2019; Eckstein & Ferris, 2018).

Our findings have implications for instruction and assessment on USF's first-year writing programme. Section 7's follow-up qualitative analysis highlighted how texts with high amod and nsubj diversity contained amod and nsubj dependencies that were used to perform a number of rhetorical functions. The connection between the association measure scores and their diverse use is important for future research. Future research needs to look at how the high- and low-scoring association measure combinations are being used to develop a sense of high or low achievement in the FYC tasks. This kind of sustained quantitative-qualitative examination would help identify how language is being used to facilitate meeting task and wider FYC programme goals. To this end, banks of authentic learner language may be invaluable for instructors as complementary aids that supplement the external 'community comments' that already exist within the My Reviewers platform.

These authentic language examples would allow instructors to clearly connect their process-oriented rhetorical instruction with examples of learner language that show students how to navigate the tasks and demonstrate ownership of their own texts. This dual approach means students receive both composition instruction and academic language support. Students should be supported to notice the wide array of language choices they have available to them in conveying their intended meaning. They should also be encouraged to make choices that are befitting of the tasks set.

8.5 Implications for Automated Scoring and Feedback Systems

The modelling work in this Element also has important implications for the possible creation of automated scoring and feedback systems on large-scale FYC programmes. There is clear opportunity to use the model equations our work is based on to inform how predictive automated systems may be trained to automatically score and give feedback on student texts (e.g., see Haberman & Sinharay, 2010). The model has important implications for the training of automated models of scoring and feedback which must balance of variables that underlie the grading process. We have modelled the influence of individual writer, task, and language status in this Element, and future training for models should be encouraged to include these variables in their work. This would be a valuable step towards modelling predictions with multiple variables in the future.

8.6 Critical Reflections and Ways Forward

It is important to interpret the study's findings with a degree of caution and awareness of the caveats that apply to the research design. A first acknowledgement is that the measurement of sophistication in the form of association measures is limited by measuring sophistication using only association measures. In the future, studies might adopt a more multidimensional approach to studying sophistication with more than one measure type. This may include looking at lists of academic collocations (e.g., in a similar manner to Paquot (2019)). The second study design decision that shapes the view of sophistication is the choice of reference corpus. While the choice of reference corpus was register appropriate for learner writing, this limited the view of sophistication by only looking at combinations present in another specialised corpus of writing, where size may have played a role in limiting the amount of language we could look at. A different picture of sophistication may be presented when the reference corpus is general in nature (e.g., use of the BNC or COCA) but it is still important to recognise that even in large general corpora multi-word units like dependencies and collocations more broadly are sometimes not found.

The study sample and our understanding of writers' first language was restricted by relying on complete responses from learners. This information was gathered via a voluntary student survey, and this means that the inferences we can draw from these learner variables are limited to having *enough* complete information. Future modelling work with big data FYC repositories like this one will need to be carried out with this issue of patchy data in mind. Although mixed effects modelling has been promoted as a statistical technique that can handle missing data, in the case of the FYC repository, there are cases where absent data is the norm, and careful consideration in future work will be needed to determine exactly the amount of missing data such modelling is able to handle. As a field, this is an issue that learner corpus research is only starting to explore and as a community it is an endeavour that should be pursued for the foreseeable future in our work (e.g., in line with recommendations made by Gries, 2015).

A further limitation relates to the exclusion of topic as a variable in the study. Students are permitted to choose their own topics, meaning that inferences and coding the variable for analysis depend on enough students choosing similar or the same topics. As a result of the idiosyncratic topic choices, grouping topics together was not possible. However, in the future the inclusion of topic as a random variable may be possible in a larger FYC sampling frame.

It is also pertinent to reflect on the limitations and caveats that apply to using cluster analysis. Although we took steps to show the validity of our working, there are several caveats that readers should be aware of. We choose a particular set of association measures, of which we accept are not an exhaustive list, but are instead one that covers multiple measures that have frequented linguistics research. Readers of other lines of word association research may uncover other measures or ponder the placement of the 'contextual measures' that we omitted for their costly calculation and infrequency in the literature we drew upon. Our clustering solution is also based on making important pre-analyses choices: the decision to scale and standardise the data to maximise the uniformity of the association measure values, the decision to employ farthest neighbour clustering, and the decision to choose spearman correlations to calculate the distance matrix. We made these decisions with reference to key statistical literature; however, other analysts who make different decisions at these junctions will no doubt obtain a slightly different clustering solution.

Similarly, there are caveats for our modelling. We opted to use cumulative links mixed effects modelling because of its ability to treat the dependent variable of 'Final_Grade' as ordinal. This aligns with other educational research (e.g., O'Connell, 2006). We hope that our approach here plays a role in the modelling conversations that are currently taking place in the movement of examining learner writing via these kinds of models because there is still much to ponder about mixed effects modelling, particularly so when managing unbalanced data sets such as the FYC one we encountered (see also McCallum, 2019).

In this light, there are several other directions that future research should be encouraged to pursue. One direction is the relationships between context-specific measures of association. While the present study opted to focus on computationally simple measures of association, there is scope for carrying out further relationship-based work that looks at how mathematically complex context measures may tap into different aspects of context and collocation properties (e.g., see Gries and Durrant's (2021) support for KL divergence as a viable candidate of study).

With respect to the context, this study represents one of the first collocation-grade studies in FYC literature, and future replications of this work across other FYC contexts would strengthen claims that instruction and assessment on these programmes would benefit from being informed by (a) corpus linguistics techniques and (b) EAP pedagogic methodologies that home in on language as a central component of composing texts.

A penultimate direction is to acknowledge that these exploratory patterns are obtained indirectly via corpus data and their interpretation is limited, if only the corpus is used, to look at the rationale for such patterns. To this end, our study should be viewed as a starting point for further qualitative exploration of the construct of writing proficiency. The patterns and language examples may be further used in psycholinguistics and interview-based research to tap into why these language examples and patterns of positive or negative relationship with writing quality scores may occur. This kind of qualitative work would act as a natural complement to the statistical and qualitative analyses carried out in this Element.

A final direction relates more broadly to the grading process. The modelling process indicates that second language writers have higher odds of a grade increase, and to some extent this quantitative heavy modelling also supports the qualitative picture built up in previous grading studies (e.g., Huang & Foote, 2010). A qualitative follow-up study on this finding may help illuminate potential trajectories of FYC rater unconscious bias.

Overall, the modelling process has illuminated several statistical patterns that should be further investigated qualitatively. This would provide a fine-grained understanding of the relationship between collocations, dependencies, and learner and contextual FYC programme variables. This is a highly viable direction that future FYC work should be encouraged to take.

References

Ackermann, K., & Chen, Y. H. (2013). Developing the academic collocation list (ACL): A corpus-driven and expert-judged approach. *Journal of English for Academic Purposes, 12*(4), 235–47.

Appel, R., & Wood, D. (2016). Recurrent word combinations in EAP test-taker writing: Differences between high and low proficiency levels. *Language Assessment Quarterly, 13*(1), 55–71.

Aull, L. L. (2015). *First-Year University Writing: A Corpus-Based Study with Implications for Pedagogy*. Palgrave Macmillan.

Aull, L. L. (2017). Corpus analysis of argumentative versus explanatory discourse in writing task genres. *Journal of Writing Analytics, 1*, 1–47.

Aull, L. L. (2019). Linguistic markers of stance and genre in upper-level student writing. *Written Communication, 36*(2), 267–95.

Baayen, H., Davidson, D., & Bates, D. (2008). Mixed effects modelling with crossed random effects for subjects and items. *Journal of Memory and Language, 59*, 390–412.

Barkaoui, K. (2008). Effects of scoring method and rater experience on ESL essay rating processes and outcomes. Unpublished Ph.D. thesis. University of Toronto.

Benson, M., Benson, E., & Ilson, R. (2009). *The BBI Combinatory Dictionary of English: Your Guide to Collocations and Grammar*. John Benjamins.

Berzak, Y., Kenney, J., Spadine, C. et al. (2016). Universal dependencies for learner English. In K. Erk & N. A. Smith, eds.. *Proceedings of the 54th Annual Meeting of the Association for Computational Linguistics*. Association for Computational Linguistics, pp. 737–46.

Bestgen, Y. (2017). Beyond single-word measures: L2 writing assessment, lexical richness and formulaic competence. *System, 69*, 65–78.

Bestgen, Y., & Granger, S. (2014). Quantifying the development of phraseological competence in L2 English writing: An automated approach. *Journal of Second Language Writing, 26*, 28–41.

Brezina, V. (2018). *Statistics for Corpus Linguistics*. Cambridge University Press.

Brezina, V., McEnery, T., & Wattam, S. (2015). Collocations in context: A new perspective on collocation networks. *International Journal of Corpus Linguistics, 20*(2), 139–73.

Brock, G., Pihur, V., Datta, S., & Datta, S. (2008). clValid: An R package for cluster validation. *Journal of Statistical Software, 25*(4), 1–22.

Brown, J. D. (1991). Do English and ESL faculties rate writing samples differently? *TESOL Quarterly*, *25*, 587–603.

Bulté, B., & Housen, A. (2014). Conceptualizing and measuring short-term changes in L2 writing complexity. *Journal of Second Language Writing*, *26*, 42–65.

Bychkovska, T., & Lee, J. J. (2017). At the same time: Lexical bundles in L1 and L2 university student argumentative writing. *Journal of English for Academic Purposes*, *30*, 38–52.

Carlson, S., & Bridgeman, B. (1986). Testing ESL student writers. In K. L. Greenberg, H. S. Weiner, & R. A. Donovan, eds., *Writing Assessment: Issues and Strategies*. Longman, pp. 126–52.

Chen, W. (2019). Profiling collocations in EFL writing of Chinese tertiary learners. *RELC Journal*, *50*(1), 53–70.

Chen, J., Zhang, M., & Bejar, I. I. (2017). An investigation of the *e-rater*® automated scoring engine's grammar, usage, mechanics, and style microfeatures and their aggregation model. *ETS Research Report Series*, 1–14. https://doi.org/10.1002/ets2.12131

Christensen, R. H. B. (2019). Ordinal: Regression Models for Ordinal Data. R package version 2019.12-10. www.cran.r-project.org/package=ordinal/

Church, K., & Hanks, P. (1990). Word association norms, mutual information and lexicography. *Computational Linguistics*, *16*, 22–9.

Council of Writing Program Administrators (CWPA), National Council of Teachers of English (NCTE), & National Writing Project (NWP). (2011). Framework for success in postsecondary writing. https://wpacouncil.org/aws/CWPA/pt/sd/news_article/242845/_PARENT/layout_details/false

Council of Writing Program Administrators (CWPA). (2014). Outcomes statement for first-year composition (3.0). https://wpacouncil.org/aws/CWPA/pt/sd/news_article/243055/_PARENT/layout_details/false

Crawley, M. J. (2013). *The R Book* (2nd ed.). Wiley.

Crossley, S. A. (2020). Linguistic features in writing quality and development: An overview. *Journal of Writing Research*, *11*(3), 415–43.

Crossley, S. A., Cai, Z., & McNamara, D. S. (2012). Syntagmatic, paradigmatic and automatic n-gram approaches to assessing essay quality. In P. M. McCarthy & G. M. Youngblood, eds., *Proceedings of the 25th International Florida Artificial Intelligence Research Society Conference*. The AAAI Press, pp. 214–19.

Daller, H., Turlik, J., & Weir, I. (2013). Vocabulary acquisition and the learning curve. In S. Jarvis & H. Daller, eds., *Vocabulary Knowledge: Human Ratings and Automated Measures*. John Benjamins, pp. 185–218.

De Marneffe, M. C., & Manning, C. D. (2008). The Stanford typed dependencies representation. In *Coling 2008: Proceedings of the Workshop on Cross-Framework and Cross-Domain Parser Evaluation.* pp. 1–8.

Debusmann, R. (2000). An introduction to dependency grammar. *Hausarbeit fur das Hauptseminar Dependenzgrammatik SoSe*, *99*, 1–16.

Dunning, T. (1993). Accurate methods for the statistics of surprise and coincidence. *Computational Linguistics*, *19*(1), 61–74.

Durrant, P. (2019). Formulaic language in English for academic purposes. In A. Siyanova-Chanturia & A. Pellicer-Sanchez, eds., *Understanding Formulaic Language: A Second Language Acquisition Perspective.* Routledge, pp. 211–28.

Durrant, P. (2020). Association measure calculator. https://phildurrant.net/association-measure-calculator/

Durrant, P., & Brenchley, M. (2021). The development of academic collocations in children's writing. In P. Szudarski & S. Barclay, eds., *Vocabulary Theory, Patterning and Teaching.* Multilingual Matters, pp. 99–120.

Durrant, P., Brenchley, M., & McCallum, L. (2021). *Understanding Development and Proficiency in Writing: Quantitative Corpus Linguistics Approaches.* Cambridge University Press.

Durrant, P., Moxley, J., & McCallum, L. (2019). Vocabulary sophistication in freshman composition assignments. *International Journal of Corpus Linguistics*, *24*(1), 31–64.

Durrant, P., & Schmitt, N. (2009). To what extent do native and non-native writers make use of collocations? *International Review of Applied Linguistics in Language Teaching*, *47*, 157–77.

Eckstein, G., & Ferris, D. (2018). Comparing L1 and L2 texts and writers in first-year composition. *TESOL Quarterly*, *52*(1), 137–62.

Eguchi, M., & Kyle, K. (2020). Continuing to explore the multidimensional nature of lexical sophistication: The case of oral proficiency interviews. *The Modern Language Journal*, *104*(2), 381–400.

Ellis, N. C. (2008). Phraseology: The periphery and the heart of language. In F. Meunier & S. Granger, eds., *Phraseology in Foreign Language Learning and Teaching.* John Benjamins, pp. 1–13.

Ellis, N. C., & Ferreira-Junior, F. (2009). Constructions and their acquisition: Islands and the distinctiveness of the occupancy. *Annual Review of Cognitive Linguistics*, *7*, 187–220.

Evert, S. (2004). The statistics of word cooccurrences: Word pairs and collocations. Unpublished Doctoral dissertation. University of Stuttgart.

Evert, S. (2009). Corpora and collocations. In A. Lüdeling & M. Kytö, eds., *Corpus Linguistics: An International Handbook* (Vol. 2). Walter de Gruyter, pp. 1212–48.

Field, A., Miles, J., & Field, Z. (2012). *Discovering Statistics Using R*. Sage.

Firth, J. R. (1957). *Papers in Linguistics 1934–1951*. Oxford University Press.

Firth, J. R. (1968). A synopsis of linguistic theory, 1930–55. In F. R. Palmer, ed., *Selected Papers of J.R. Firth 1952–1959*. Longman, pp. 168–205.

Gablasova, D., Brezina, V., & McEnery, T. (2017a). Collocations in corpus-based language learning research: Identifying, comparing and interpreting the evidence. *Language Learning*, *67*, 155–79.

Gablasova, D., Brezina, V., & McEnery, T. (2017b). MI-score-based collocations in language learning research: A critical evaluation. Paper presented at the Corpus Linguistics conference at the University of Birmingham.

Garner, J., Crossley, S., & Kyle, K. (2019). Ngrams and L2 writing proficiency. *System*, *80*, 176–87.

Garner, J., Crossley, S., & Kyle, K. (2020). Beginning and intermediate L2 writer's use of ngrams: An association measures study. *International Review of Applied Linguistics*, *58*(1), 51–74.

Granger, S., & Bestgen, Y. (2014). The use of collocations by intermediate vs. advanced non-native writers: A bigram-based study. *International Review of Applied Linguistics*, *52*(3), 229–52.

Granger, G., & Paquot, M. (2008). Disentangling the phraseological web. In S. Granger & F. Meunier, eds., *Phraseology: An Interdisciplinary Perspective*. John Benjamins, pp. 27–49.

Granger, G., & Paquot, M. (2009). Lexical verbs in academic discourse: A corpus-driven study of learner use. In M. Charles, D. Pecorari, & S. Hunston, eds., *Academic Writing: At the Interface of Corpus and Discourse*. Continuum, pp. 193–214.

Gries, S. T. (2013a). 50-something years of work on collocations: What is or should be next. *International Journal of Corpus Linguistics*, *18*(1), 137–65.

Gries, S. T. (2013b). *Statistics for Linguists with R: A Practical Introduction* (2nd revised ed.). De Gruyter Mouton.

Gries, S. T. (2015). The most under-used statistical method in corpus linguistics: Multi-level (and mixed effects) models. *Corpora*, *10*(1), 95–126.

Gries, S. T., & Durrant, P. (2021). Analysing co-occurrence data. In S. Gries & M. Paquot, eds., *A Practical Handbook of Corpus Linguistics*. Springer, pp. 141–59.

Gries, S. T., & Ellis, N. C. (2015). Statistical measures for usage-based linguistics. *Language Learning*, *65*(S1), 228–55.

Guo, L., Crossley, S. A., & McNamara, D. S. (2013). Predicting human judgements of essay quality in both integrated and independent second language writing samples: A comparison study. *Assessing Writing*, *18*, 218–38.

Haberman, S. J., & Sinharay, S. (2010). The application of the cumulative logistic regression model to automated essay scoring. *Journal of Educational and Behavioral Statistics*, *35*(5), 586–602.

Hawkins, J. A., & Filipovic, L. (2012). *Criterial Features in L2 English: Specifying the Reference Levels of the Common European Framework*. Cambridge University Press.

Henriksen, B. (2013). Research on L2 learners' collocational competence and development: A progress report. In C. Bardel, C. Lindqvist, & B. Laufer, eds., *L2 Vocabulary Acquisition, Knowledge and Use: New Perspectives on Assessment and Corpus Analysis*. EuroSLA, pp. 29–56.

Hoey, M. (1991). *Patterns of Lexis in Text*. Oxford University Press.

Hoey, M. (2005). *Lexical Priming: A New Theory of Words and Language*. Routledge.

Hosmer, D. W., & Lemeshow, S. (2000). *Applied Logistic Regression*. Wiley.

Hou, J., Verspoor, M., & Loerts, H. (2016). An exploratory study into the dynamics of Chinese L2 writing development. *Dutch Journal of Applied Linguistics*, *5*(1), 65–96.

Hox, J. (2002). *Multilevel Analysis: Techniques and Applications*. Lawrence Erlbaum.

Huang, J., & Foote, C. J. (2010). Grading between lines: What really impacts professors' holistic evaluation of ESL graduate student writing? *Language Assessment Quarterly*, *7*(3), 219–33.

Huang, Y., Murakami, A., Alexopoulou, T., & Korhonen, A. (2018). Dependency parsing of learner English. *International Journal of Corpus Linguistics*, *23*(1), 28–54.

Jeffery, J. V., & Wilcox, K. C. (2013). How do I do it if I don't like writing? Adolescents' stance toward writing across disciplines. *Reading & Writing*, *27*(6), 1095–117.

Jiang, J., Bi, P., Xie, N., & Liu, H. (2021). Phraseological complexity and low- and intermediate-level L2 learners' writing quality. *International Review of Applied Linguistics in Language Teaching*. https://doi.org/10.1515/iral-2019-0147

Jones, S., & Sinclair, J. M. (1974). English lexical collocations: A study in computational linguistics. *Cahiers de Lexicologie*, *24*, 15–61.

Kim, J. (2014). Predicting L2 writing proficiency using linguistic complexity measures: A corpus-based study. *English Teaching*, *69*(4), 27–51.

Kim, M., Crossley, S. A., & Kyle, K. (2018). Lexical sophistication as a multidimensional phenomenon: Relations to second language lexical proficiency, development and writing quality. *The Modern Language Journal*, *102*(1), 120–41.

Kyle, K. (2020). The relationship between features of source text use and integrated writing quality. *Assessing Writing, 45*, 1–12. https://doi.org/10.1016/j.asw.2020.100467

Kyle, K. (2021). Natural language processing for learner corpus research. *International Journal of Learner Corpus Research, 7*(1), 1–16. https://doi.org/10.1075/ijlcr.00019.int

Kyle, K., & Crossley, S. A. (2016). The relationship between lexical sophistication and independent and source-based writing. *Journal of Second Language Writing, 34*, 12–24.

Kyle, K., Crossley, S. A., & Berger, C. (2018). The tool for the analysis of lexical sophistication (TAALES): Version 2.0. *Behavior Research Methods, 50*(3), 1030–46. https://doi.org/10.3758/s13428-017-0924-4

Kyle, K., Crossley, S., & Verspoor, M. (2021). Measuring longitudinal writing development using indices of syntactic complexity and sophistication. *Studies in Second Language Acquisition, 43*(4), 781–812. https://doi.org/10.1017/S0272263120000546

Kyle, K., & Eguchi, M. (2021). Automatically assessing lexical sophistication using word, bigram, and dependency indices. In S. Granger, ed., *Perspectives on the Second Language Phrasicon: The View from Learner Corpora*. Multilingual Matters, 126–151. www.multilingual-matters.com/page/detail/?k=9781788924863

Lee, J. (2019). A comparison of writing tasks in ESL writing and first-year composition courses: A case study of one university. *Language Teaching Research, 25*(3), 1–18.

Levshina, N. (2015). *How to Do Linguistics with R: Data Exploration and Statistical Analysis*. John Benjamins.

Liu, X. (2016). *Applied Ordinal Logistic Regression Using Stata: From Single-level to Multilevel Modeling*. Sage.

Llanes, À., Tragant, E., & Serrano, R. (2018). Examining the role of learning context and individual differences in gains in L2 writing performance: The case of teenagers on an intensive study-abroad programme. *The Language Learning Journal, 46*(2), 201–16. DOI:10.1080/09571736.2015.1020332

Loerts, H., Lowie, W., & Seton, B. (2020). *Essential Statistics for Applied Linguistics: Using R or JASP*. Bloomsbury.

Lorenzo, F., & Rodríguez, L. (2014). Onset and expansion of L2 cognitive academic language proficiency in bilingual settings: CALP in CLIL. *System, 47*, 64–72.

Maechler, M., Rousseeuw, P., Struyf, A., Hubert, M., & Hornik, K. (2015). Cluster: Cluster analysis basics and extensions. R package version 2.0.1.

Manning, C. D., Surdeanu, M., Bauer, J. et al. (2014). The Stanford CoreNLP natural language processing toolkit. In K. Bontcheva., & J. Zhu, eds., *Proceedings of the 52nd Annual Meeting of the Association for Computational Linguistics: System Demonstrations.* Association for Computational Linguistics, pp. 55–60.

Marcus, M., Marcinkiewicz, M., & Santorini, B. (1993). Building a large annotated corpus of English: The Penn Treebank. *Computational Linguistics, 19*, 313–30.

Matsuda, P. K., Saenkhum, T., & Accardi, S. (2013). Writing teachers' perceptions of the presence and needs of second language writers: An institutional case study. *Journal of Second Language Writing, 22*, 68–86.

McCallum, L. (2019). Modelling score variation in student writing with a big data system: Benefits, challenges, and ways forward. *Journal of Writing Analytics, 3*, 286–311.

McCallum, L. (2021). The role of lexical collocations and learner and course variables in determining writing quality in assignments from a first year composition programme. Unpublished EdD thesis. University of Exeter.

Michigan Corpus of Upper-Level Student Papers (MICUSP). (2009). MICUSP Fair Use https://micusp.elicorpora.info/

Moore, T., & Morton, J. (2005). Dimensions of difference: A comparison of university writing and IELTS writing. *Journal of English for Academic Purposes, 4*(1), 43–66.

Moxley, J. M., & Eubanks, D. (2015). On keeping score: Instructors' vs. students' rubric ratings of 46,689 essays. *Writing Program Administration, 39*(2), 53–80.

Nesselhauf, N. (2005). *Collocations in a Learner Corpus.* Studies in Corpus Linguistics (Vol. 14). John Benjamins.

O'Connell, A. A. (2006). *Logistic Regression Models for Ordinal Response Variables.* Sage.

Öksuz, D., Brezina, V., & Rebuschat, P. (2021). Collocational processing in L1 and L2: The effects of word frequency, collocational frequency, and association. *Language Learning, 71*(1), 55–98.

Osgood, C. E. (1952). The nature and measurement of meaning. *Psychological Bulletin, 49*, 197–237.

Paquot, M. (2018). The phraseological dimension in interlanguage complexity research. *Second Language Research, 35*(1), 121–45.

Paquot, M. (2019). Phraseological competence: A useful toolbox to delimitate CEFR levels in higher education? Insights from a study of EFL learners' use of statistical collocations. *Language Assessment Quarterly, 15*(1), 29–43.

Pecina, P. (2005). An extensive empirical study of collocation extraction methods. In *Proceedings of the ACL Student Research Workshop.* pp. 13–18.

Pecina, P. (2010). Lexical association measures and collocation extraction. *Language Resources & Evaluation*, *44*, 137–58.

Picoral, A., Staples, S., & Reppen, R. (2021). Automated annotation of learner English: An evaluation of software tools. *International Journal of Learner Corpus Research*, *7*(1), 17–52.

University of South Florida (USF). (2018). Points of Pride USF. www.usf.edu/about-usf/points-of-pride.aspx

Quellmalz, E. S., Capell, F. J., & Chov, C. P. (1982). Effects of discourse and response mode on the measurement of writing competence. *Journal of Educational Measurement*, *19*, 241–58.

R Core Development Team. (2014). R: A language and environment for statistical computing. R Foundation for Statistical Computing. www.R-project.org

Römer, U. (2009). English in academia: Does nativeness matter? *Anglistik*: *International Journal of English Studies*, *20*, 89–100.

Römer, U., & O'Donnell, M. B. (2011). From student hard drive to web corpus (part 1): The design, compilation and genre classification of the Michigan Corpus of Upper-level Student Papers (MICUSP). *Corpora*, *6*(2), 159–77.

Ruth, L., & Murphy, S. (1988). *Designing Writing Tasks for the Assessment of Writing*. Ablex.

Schmitt, N., & Schmitt, D. (2020). *Vocabulary in Language Learning* (2nd ed.). Cambridge University Press.

Schneider, U. (2020). ΔP as a measure of collocation strength: Considerations based on analyses of hesitation placement in spontaneous speech. *Corpus Linguistics and Linguistic Theory*, *16*(2), 249–74.

Seretan, V. (2011). *Syntax-Based Collocation Extraction: Text, Speech and Language Technology Series* (Vol. 44). Springer Science and Business Media. https://doi.org/10.1007/978-94-007-0134-2_4

Sinclair, J. M. (1987). Collocation: A progress report. In R. Steele & T. Threadgold, eds., *Language Topics: Essays in Honour of Michael Halliday* (Vol. 2). John Benjamins, pp. 319–31.

Sinclair, J. (1991). *Corpus, Concordance, Collocation*. Oxford University Press.

Siyanova-Chanturia, A., & Pellicer-Sánchez, A. (2019). Formulaic language: Setting the scene. In A. Siyanova-Chanturia & A. Pellicer-Sánchez, eds., *Understanding Formulaic Language*. Routledge, pp. 1–15.

Smadja, F. (1993). Retrieving collocations from text: Xtract. *Computational Linguistics*, *19*(1), 143–77.

Tabachnick, B. G., & Fidell, L. S. (2014). *Using Multivariate Statistics* (6th ed.). Pearson Education Limited.

Tedick, D. (1990). ESL writing assessment: Subject-matter knowledge and its impact on performance. *English for Specific Purposes*, *9*, 123–43.

Treffers-Daller, J., Parslow, P., & Williams, S. (2018). Back to basics: How measures of lexical diversity can help discriminate between CEFR Levels. *Applied Linguistics*, *39*(3), 302–27.

Verspoor, M., Lowie, M., Chan, H. P., & Vahtrick, L. (2017). Linguistic complexity in second language development: Variability and variation at advanced stages. *Recherches en didactique des langues et des cultures*, *14*(1), 1–28.

Ward, J. (2007). Collocation and technicality in EAP engineering. *Journal of English for Academic Purposes*, *6*(1), 18–35.

Weigle, S. C. (1999). Investigating rater/prompt interactions in writing assessment: Quantitative and qualitative approaches. *Assessing Writing*, *6*, 145–78.

Wiechmann, D. (2008). On the computation of collostruction strength: Testing measures of association as expressions of lexical bias. *Corpus Linguistics and Linguistic Theory*, *4*(2), 253–90.

Winter, B. (2020). *Statistics for Linguists: An Introduction Using R*. Routledge.

Wray, A. (2002). *Formulaic Language and the Lexicon*. Cambridge University Press.

Wray, A. (2006). Formulaic language. In K. Brown, ed., *Encyclopedia of Language and Linguistics* (Vol. 4). Elsevier, pp. 590–7.

Wray, A. (2019). Concluding question: Why don't second language learners more proactively target formulaic sequences? In A. Siyanova-Chanturia & A. Pellicer-Sánchez, eds., *Understanding Formulaic Language*. Routledge, pp. 248–69.

Acknowledgements

The data used in this Element were obtained as part of a wider programme of work on the My Reviewers 'My R' database. We therefore fully acknowledge that our data were compiled from the My R databases hosted in the Department of English at the University of South Florida. Our research was approved under USF IRB No. Pro00021265. The work was also supported by a University of Exeter/University of South Florida grant under the Doctoral Catalyst scheme.

Cambridge Elements ☰

Corpus Linguistics

Susan Hunston
University of Birmingham

Professor of English Language at the University of Birmingham, UK. She has been involved in Corpus Linguistics for many years and has written extensively on corpora, discourse, and the lexis-grammar interface. She is probably best known as the author of Corpora in Applied Linguistics (2002, Cambridge University Press). Susan is currently co-editor, with Carol Chapelle, of the Cambridge Applied Linguistics series.

Advisory Board
Professor Paul Baker, *Lancaster University*
Professor Jesse Egbert, *Northern Arizona University*
Professor Gaetanelle Gilquin, *Université Catholique de Louvain*

About the Series
Corpus Linguistics has grown to become part of the mainstream of Linguistics and Applied Linguistics, as well as being used as an adjunct to other forms of discourse analysis in a variety of fields. It continues to become increasingly complex, both in terms of the methods it uses and in relation to the theoretical concepts it engages with. The Cambridge Elements in Corpus Linguistics series has been designed to meet the needs of both students and researchers who need to keep up with this changing field. The series includes introductions to the main topic areas by experts in the field as well as accounts of the latest ideas and developments by leading researchers.

Cambridge Elements ☰

Corpus Linguistics

Printed in the United States
by Baker & Taylor Publisher Services